Z-kai
Zoom-Up Workbook

Math

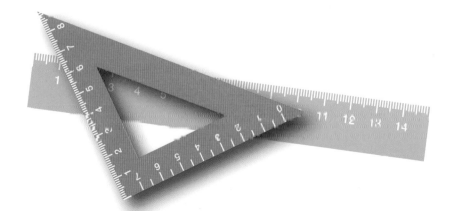

Grade 5

Introduction

— Z-kai Values Thinking Skills and a Disposition for Learning —

Z-kai's **Zoom-Up Workbook** is tailored to develop students' mathematical thinking, problem solving, and explanation skills that are necessary for their future success in STEM. This series contains many problems that challenge students, because the problem solving requires them to apply mathematical concepts and develop skills that are uncommon to the mathematics curricula and instruction of most schools and classrooms. This series was developed to reflect or surpass grade-specific Common Core State Standards in Mathematics (CCSS-M, 2010). The application of mathematical reasoning, problem solving, and explaining mathematics provides multiple opportunities for students to apply the CCSS-M Standards for Mathematical Content and Practice.

Z-kai offers educational services in Japan from its inception in 1931, particularly focused on developing challenging material for advanced and gifted PreK-12 students. Z-kai's extensive experience helped the company focus on students' developing two important lifelong learning skills: (1) problem solving, reasoning, and flexible thinking; and (2) a disposition for curiosity, independent study and research, and collaboration with others to solve challenging problems. Through experiences educating more than 200,000 Japanese students each year, Z-kai has learned that it is better for students to solve a limited number of well-thought-out problems rather than numerous less-challenging ones. In this way, students' mathematical knowledge, thinking skills, and processing are maximized and made more flexible.

This Zoom-Up Workbook contains 45 challenging problem sets that have been carefully selected to optimize students' understanding and perseverance. Given a limited number of total problems, the focus is on depth of understanding rather than breadth of completion. Solving challenging tasks will help students develop confidence and motivation.

Another strength of Zoom-Up Workbooks is that many of the problems relate to the daily life of students. Applying previously-learned mathematics knowledge and skills to solve problems of daily living helps students to see mathematics as useful and effective. Just as importantly, students develop interest and an eagerness for applying mathematics in their daily lives.

**Solving challenging story problems develops students' mathematical practice that is necessary
for success in middle school and beyond.**

This workbook aims not only to build knowledge of algebra and geometry, but also to develop the following mathematical practice:

- Problem Solving Skills: Looking for necessary prior knowledge and utilizing this knowledge to solve new problem(s) that students have not yet learned to solve.
- Reading, Comprehension, and Representation Skills: Comprehending mathematics problem situations and representing them in diagrams, tables, graphs, and expressions.
- Explanation Skills: Explaining and justifying mathematical thinking processes and solutions.
- Comparison and Generalization Skills: Finding effective, better, and more efficient solution processes.

These skills are required in middle school and upper-level mathematics; therefore, it is important to refine and solidify these skills during the elementary school years.

How to use Z-kai Zoom-Up Workbook

1 This Zoom-Up Workbook contains 45 problem sets. We recommend that you solve problems starting with the first problem set (Problem 01) in the workbook. The problems are challenging, so please take your time and don't easily give up on finding the solutions. It might take a few days to solve each problem set them.

2 After you finish one problem set, check your answers by referring to the pages in the "Answers and Solutions" section at the back of the workbook.
If your answer is wrong, please read carefully "How to think and Solve" and review the problem.

3 If an answer is incorrect, carefully read the section "How to Think and Solve" before reviewing your solution process. It is a good idea not to erase any mistakes in your work. Instead, use a different colored pen or pencil to make corrections and/or make notes to explain your mistakes and how you corrected your thinking. By doing this, you will more clearly understand and remember the mathematics needed to solve the problem(s).

4 In each section titled "If you know this, the math-and-you are cool!" or "It's awesome if you know!," you will find useful information that will help you understand and increase your learning.

5 The problems marked with the thumbs-up symbol 👍 are very challenging problems. When you figure out how to solve these problems, you should be very proud of your achievement.

Dear parents, Dear teachers,

The Z-kai Zoom-Up Workbook is designed for students to be able to work independently. The workbook provides an "Answers and Solutions" section that gives detailed explanations about how to think about and understand challenging problem solutions. To develop good habits for learning mathematics' problem solving, we recommend that students check and compare their answers and solution process to the material in "Answers and Solutions." We also encourage parents and teachers to read the explanations together with students, especially since reading and comprehending explanations is challenging for all students, at least some of the time.

Since everyone should learn to enjoy the challenge of thinking about and solving challenging problems … let's solve challenging problems together!

Eamal   Milmali   Iwanko

Z-kai Zoom-Up Workbook Math Grade 5

1 Today is September 1st. Benjamin is a new 5th grade student. He likes Mathematics. He is now trying to solve digital clock number puzzles.

Ⓐ Ten numerals are used in the digital clock. Find all numerals that can be read as numbers even when you rotate them to an upside down position. (20 points)

(   )

Ⓑ Using the numbers listed above, we will make three-digit numbers. How many three-digit numbers can be read as the same three-digit number even when you rotate the book so the number is turned upside down? You can use the same number as many times as you like. (30 points)

(   )

> **Hint**
>
> When you turn a three-digit number upside down, the number in the ones place becomes the number in the hundreds place. So, be sure to pay attention to the numerals in the ones and in the hundreds places. You might miss some three-digit pairs, so investigate each one carefully.

Ⓒ A digital clock shows the date and time, as shown below:

When the numbers for the month, day, hour, minute, or second are single-digit numbers, a zero (0) must be placed in the tens place.

Benjamin is investigating date and time combinations that use all numerals from 0 to 9 only once, such as "07 23 19 56 48." What is the earliest date and time in a year that uses all numbers from 0 to 9 only once? (50 points)

(   )

We are thinking about the earliest date and time in a year, so it is a good idea to start investigating from January. It is important to keep in mind that the digital clock cannot show times such as 45 hours or 89 seconds.

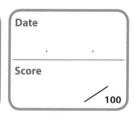

Date

Score

/ 100

1 Benjamin and his father went to a beach and collected many seashells.

Ⓐ Benjamin's father placed seashells on the sand in the following way:

RULE

Put one seashell in the first row.
In the second row add two more shells.
Continue adding two more shells to
each new row.

Benjamin and his father are discussing a better way to find the total number of seashells if he continues to place seashells following the rule above.

Benjamin's father: Let's find the sum of the seashells we've placed through the fourth row. For example, what if we imagine another set of four rows of seashells that follow the same rule? Then we can combine this second set with the original, as shown below. What do you notice?

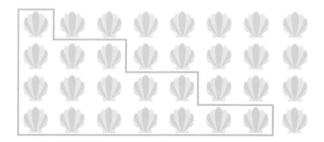

Benjamin: It forms a rectangle! The number of seashells we want to find will be half the total number of seashells in the rectangle. ... So, we can use multiplication and division to find the number of seashells.

How many seashells are there through the first to the fourth row? Use multiplication and division to find the number of the seashells. (15 points for the math sentence, 15 points for the answer)

Math Sentence

Answer ( )

B Benjamin is thinking about how many seashells he needs if he makes 50 rows of seashells. First, find how many seashells will be in the 50th row. Then find how many seashells he will need to make 50 rows of seashells. (15 points each)

The number of seashells in the 50th row ( )

Total number of seashells ( )

2 Benjamin's mother gave Benjamin a challenging math problem. Think of a better way to solve this problem. (40 points)

Given the whole numbers 1 through 1000, what is the sum of all numbers that produce a remainder of 3 when the number is divided by 4?

Hint

First, find and record all the numbers that when divided by 4 have a remainder of 3. It will be fantastic if you can think about using a strategy that is similar to the strategy we used in Problem 1

1 September 12th is Space Day in Japan. On September 12, 1992, the astronaut Mamoru "Mark" Mohri became the first Japanese astronaut to go into space aboard the Space Shuttle Endeavour. Reiko and Haruto are talking about space while browsing a book about space and space travel.

Reiko: The book says the distance between the earth and the sun is about 149,600,000 km.

Haruto: I wonder how long it would take to travel on the Shinkansen (the bullet train) from the earth to the sun.

Reiko: To make the calculation easy, let's think about the speed of Shinkansen as 300 km per hour. Also, let's approximate the distance from the earth to the sun by rounding the distance to the highest two place values.

Hatuto: The math sentence will be (①), so we can say that it will take (②) hours.

Reiko: If we change the time in hours to time in years, it will take about 60 years. The distance between the earth and the sun is so far away, it is unimaginable.

Haruto: This book mentioned the speed of light. Light can travel about 300,000 km in 1 second. Wow, that is so fast! If we compare the speed of light to the speed of the Shinkansen, the speed of light is (③) times as much.

Reiko: The distance that light can travel in a calendar year is called a "light year." The expanse of space is so monumental that we cannot use familiar distance units, such as kilometers and meters. So, if we measure the distance in outer space, we need to use the "light year" unit.

Haruto: Because we measure 1 year as 365 days on earth, I wonder how many kilometers light will have traveled in one light year?

Reiko: Well, even though the multiplication seems difficult, let's do our best to calculate. The math sentence will be (④), so the distance is (⑤) km.

Ⓐ We are going to find out how long it will take to travel from the earth to the sun on the Shinkansen. Please write an apocopate math sentence for ①. Then find an appropriate number for ②. (10 points each)

(①) (   )   (②) (   )

B We are comparing the distance light travels in 1 minute to find out how many times faster the speed of light is compared to thc the speed of the Shinkansen. Find an appropriate number for ③. (20 points)

(③) ( )

C We are finding how many km are in 1 light year. Write an appropriate math sentence for ④. Please round the answer number ⑤ to the highest two places. (10 points each)

(④) [ ]

(⑤) ( )

D The distance between the earth and the sun is called one "astronomical unit." How many "astronomical units" is 1 light year? Before calculating the distance between the earth and the sun in km and in 1 light year found in problem **C**, round to the highest two places. Round the answer to the highest two places, also. (20 points for the math sentence, 20 points for the answer)

Math Sentence

Answer ( )

It's awesome if you know!

The distance of 1 astronomical unit is the distance light travels in about 8 minutes. So the light from the sun takes about 8 minutes to get to the earth. If we travel on the Shinkansen, it will take about 60 years, because the speed of light is so fast. When you research space, you will find many large numbers. It is so very interesting. Please go to the library at your school or in your town or city and do more research.

1 Rachel has a CD and a DVD. On the CD, it says "700 MB" and on the DVD, it says "4.7 GB." Rachel is interested to know what 700MB and 4.7 GB means. So, she went to the school library to do some research. The summary of her research is given below.

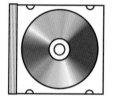

- To show the size of data created on a computer or the capacity of data on recording devices the unit "B" is used. It is read as "byte."
- 1B is the data size of one numeral or one alphabet letter. Japanese characters such as hiragana (e.g., あ、い、う) and kanji (e.g. 東、西) are more complex characters than alphabet letters, so a character uses 2B.
- 1000B is equal to 1kB and read it as "1 kilobyte."
- MB is read as "megabyte" and 1MB = 1000kB
- GB is read as "gigabyte" and 1GB = 1000MB

Ⓐ How many B (bytes) is equal to 1 GB (gigabyte)? (20 points)

( )

Ⓑ A sentence "１２本のHB鉛筆"has 8 characters. (The expression stands for "twelve HB pencils.") How many B is the size of these 8 characters? (20 points)

( )

C The sizes of data needed to record a photo, a video, or music are much larger than a text file. Rachel is thinking about recording photo data on to a 700 MB CD. If the size of a photo is 3MB, how many photos can she record on the CD?
(15 points for the math sentence, 15 points for the answer)

Math Sentence

Answer  (   )

D Rachel's father wants to record a 1 hour 10-minute video of the school musical at Rachel's school. To record the video on his video camera he needs to use an SD card. So, Racheal's father went to a camera store to find out more. If the size of a 1-minute movie is 112MB, which size SD card is appropriate for him to purchase from the following SD cards A - E? Choose all the SD cards you think are appropriate for him to purchase.
(30 points)

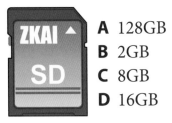

A 128GB
B 2GB
C 8GB
D 16GB

(   )

 TB ("terabyte") is used for showing the size of even larger-sized data sets.
1 TB = 1000GB
A TB is equivalent to 1 trillion B. If we could learn even more about different units that would be fun!

5 Let's Measure Time Wisely! (Part 1)

Date

.   .

Score

/100

1 Sarah found two hourglasses (sand timers) when she was cleaning a classroom. She brought them to show her teacher, Mr. Turner. They are talking about how they can measure various lengths of time using these two hourglasses.

Mr. Turner: One of the hourglasses measures 5 minutes and the other one measures 8 minutes. What lengths of time can you measure using these two hourglasses?

Sarah: They are 5-minute and 8-minute hourglasses, so we can measure 5 and 8 minutes.

Mr. Turner: That's right, but you could also measure other different lengths of time using both hourglasses together.

Sarah: Really?

Mr. Turner: For example, first make sure both hourglasses have all the sand in the bottom. Then imagine flipping both hourglasses simultaneously (at the very same moment). When the sand in the 5-minute hourglass runs out, flip it over immediately. Now start to measure the time from that moment until the sand of the 8-minute hourglass runs out. How many minutes of time have you measured?

Sarah: Well…, I can measure ① [   ] minutes.

Mr. Turner: Well done! Let's continue with the five-minute hourglass still running. Flip the 8-minute hourglass as soon as its sand runs out. Start measuring the time at that moment. If we measure time until the sand of the 5-minute hourglass runs out, how many minutes of time will we have measured?

Sarah: ② [   ] minutes.

Mr Turner: Exactly! Now, you know how to measure lengths of time other than 5 and 8 minutes using these two hourglasses.

Ⓐ Fill in the appropriate numbers in the [   ] (20 points each)

14

B Sarah is thinking about how she could measure various different times with these two hourglasses. So she decided to continue to flip the hourglasses as soon as the sand runs out. She made a diagram showing how the two hourglasses are flipped, as shown below.

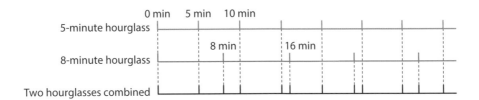

Please explain how she can measure 6 minutes. (30 points)

C We continue to flip the hourglasses to measure time as Sarah did in problem **B**. Counting from the first time she flips the second hourglass, how many minutes will it take to see the following eight lengths of time: 1, 2, 3, 4, 5, 6, 7, and 8 minutes? (30 points)

If you can solve this, the math – and you – are cool!

If we draw a diagram and use it to think, the problem is easier to figure out and the solution looks cool, too!

15

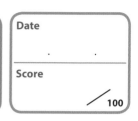

Date

·   ·

Score

/100

1 Calculate the following. If the calculation is not divisible, find the quotient as a whole number and show any remainders. (10 points each)

A
$46 \overline{)92}$

B
$34 \overline{)79}$

C
$26 \overline{)88}$

D
$11 \overline{)82}$

E
$13 \overline{)85}$

F
$15 \overline{)93}$

G
$22 \overline{)91}$

H
$14 \overline{)78}$

2 Put appropriate numbers in the ☐s below. (5 points each)

A
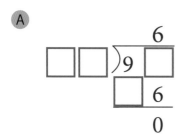

B
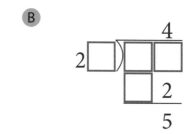

3 What numbers go in the ☐s below if the quotient is a 2-digit number? Find all the numbers that satisfy this condition. (5 points each)

A
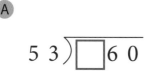

B
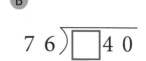

(   )   (   )

For Ⓐ above, compare the sizes of ☐60 and 53.

17

Date

Score

/100

1 Calculate the following. If the calculation is not divisible, find the quotient as a whole number and show any remainders. (10 points each)

Ⓐ

$45\overline{)315}$

Ⓑ

$76\overline{)684}$

Ⓒ

$52\overline{)460}$

Ⓓ

$45\overline{)990}$

Ⓔ

$35\overline{)952}$

Ⓕ

$23\overline{)872}$

Ⓖ

$123\overline{)622}$

Ⓗ

$32\overline{)5975}$

18

2 Put appropriate numbers in the ☐s. (5 points each)

Ⓐ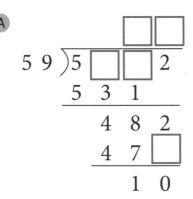

Ⓑ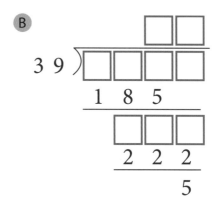

3 I was going to divide a number by 8, but mistakenly I divided it by 6! That gave me the quotient 83 and remainder 5. Find the quotient and the remainder of the correct calculation I intended to make.   (10 points)

(   )

Represent the unknown number with ☐ and write the sentence that shows the mistaken calculation. Think about how to check a division calculation when there is a remainder.

8   Let's Measure Time Wisely! (Part 2)

1 There is an incense stick that burns for 20 minutes. Let's think about how to measure time by using this stick.

We can simply measure 20 minutes because it burns for 20 minutes.
Let's think about the case when both sides of the incense stick are lit at the same time. In this case, the stick will burn in half the time, 10 minutes. So we can measure 10-minute lengths of time.

A Explain how to measure 15 minutes by using two 20-minute incense sticks. (20 points)

$$\left[\right]$$

> **Hint**
>
> Consider the previous case of measuring 10 minutes. Think about when and where you want to light the two incense sticks.

B What 5-minute time intervals from 5 to 60 minutes (e.g., 5, 10, 15, ..., 60) cannot be measured using three or less than three 20-minute incense sticks? Write all the times that cannot be measured. (30 points)

$$( )$$

20

2 There are three kinds of incense sticks that burn for 2 minutes, 3 minutes, or 6 minutes. We are going to think about measuring time using these three incense sticks.

A You will measure 1 minute using one of the three incense sticks. Explain how you can measure 1 minute. (20 points)

Think about this problem using ideas you learned from solving previous problems.

B You will measure 10 minutes by using all three incense sticks. Explain how you can measure 10 minutes. (30 points)

1 Ms. Evans and Natalia are talking about a geometry puzzle.

> A rectangle is made up of 2 rows of 5 squares.
> Split the rectangle into two identical shapes (make sure you use the dotted lines as a guide to splitting the original rectangle).
> If these two shapes exactly match each other when flipped and/or rotated, then this is one way of splitting the rectangle.

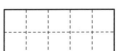

Natalia : I found 2 ways to divide the rectangle. Are these all the ways the rectangle can be split into two?

(Figure A) (Figure B)

 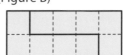

Ms. Evans : There is one more way to split the rectangle. Be careful, because if you turn and flip the pieces in figure (B) the two pieces match and are the same. So, this way of splitting the shape (as shown below) is not a different way.

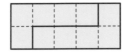

Ⓐ Find one more way to split the rectangle. Draw lines to show how you split the rectangle. (20 points)

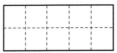

Natalia : There are only three ways to split a rectangle with two rows of five squares. If we don't start with this rectangle, there are many ways to connect 5 squares.

Ms. Evans : Yes. Let's think about what kinds of five-square figures are possible. It should be very interesting to investigate.

22

B   In addition to figures (A) and (B) shown to the left, there are 10 more figures made up of 5 squares. Draw all the figures in the grid below. Figures with squares that are connected only at a point will not be included, such as figure (C) shown below. If one shape exactly matches another shape when it is flipped or rotated, the shapes will be considered the same. (8 points etch)

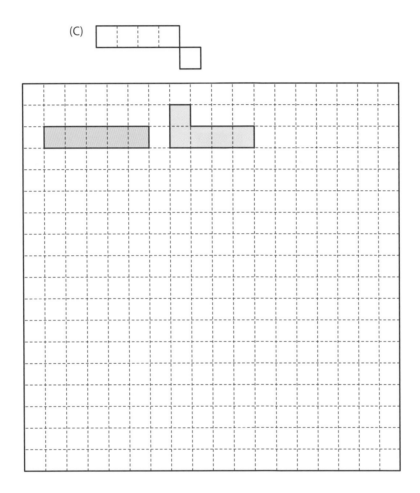

The figure you found in Ⓐ is one of the figures you are looking for.

Hint

Focus on the number of squares that are connected horizontally and use that to think in an organized manner about what to do next. For example, figure (B) has 4 squares connected horizontally.

23

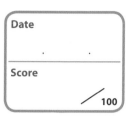

1 We found 12 different figures made up of 5 squares, as shown below.

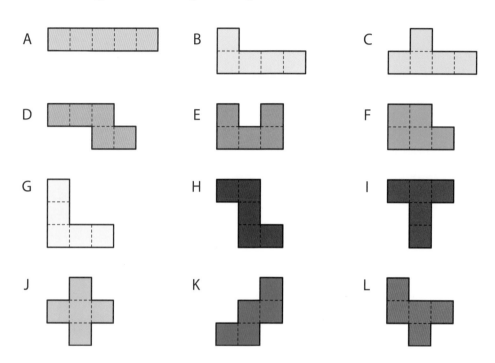

A Can you completely fill a rectangle made up of 3 rows of 5 squares using the combinations of three figures given below? You may flip or rotate the figures to fill the rectangle. Put a √ mark to indicate which combinations work. (10 points each)

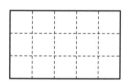

① The figures B, D and G ( )

② The figures F, I and L ( )

③ The figures H, J and K ( )

④ The figures C, E, and F ( )

B Even if you use figures A to L multiple times and flip and rotate the figures, it's impossible to fill a rectangle made up of 4 rows of 6 squares. Explain why this is impossible.
(30 points)

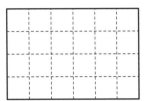

Hint

Pay attention to the area you need to cover. If you think about the area of one square as 1 cm², …

C The rectangle below is made up of 3 rows of 20 squares, and it is already filled with the figures G, H, C, and K. Fill the rectangle completely using the rest of the 8 figures only once. You can flip and rotate the figures. (30 points)

★It's awesome if you know!★

Pentominos

Pentominos are shapes that are composed of 5 connected squares. There are 12 different figures as shown in figures A to L in the previous problem. (If we include figures that are flips or rotations of B, C, D, and H, there are a total of 18 figures.)

We use the 12 figures only once to fill the rectangle in problem C above. In the same way, we can also fill rectangles with 4 rows of 15 squares, 5 rows of 12 squares, and 6 rows of 10 squares.

If we consider figures that are the same when they are flipped or rotated, there are 2 ways to fill the 3 rows of 20 squares rectangle. As for the rectangle made up of 6 rows of 10 squares, there are 2,339 ways to fill it!

1 Benjamin is a calculation champion. He discovered a very interesting fact about multiples.

Ⓐ The notes below show what Benjamin summarized about his discovery. Fill in the ⬜ below with appropriate numbers and verify whether Benjamin's discovery is correct. If boxes are labeled with the same number (1, 2, or 3), then the numbers within those boxes should also be the same. (20 points each)

< My Discovery >
Six-digit numbers made up of repeating three-digit numbers, such as 123,123, are always multiples of 7.

< My Reason>
For example, 123,123 can be decomposed into 123,000 and 123.
123,123 = 123,000 + 123

$$= 123 \times (\boxed{①} + 1)$$

$$= 123 \times \boxed{②}$$

So, 123,123 is a multiple of $\boxed{②}$.

$$\boxed{②} \div 7 = \boxed{③}$$

From this calculation we can say that $\boxed{②}$ can be divided by 7; therefore, we can say that 123,123 is a multiple of 7.

I can explain other six-digit numbers in the same way.
If a six-digit number is represented as ABCABC, the math sentence can be written as ABCABC = ABC $\times \boxed{②}$ just as we did with 123,123.

Ⓑ Benjamin also discovered the following, stated below.

< My Discovery >
Any six-digit number made up of three repetitions of a two-digit number (such as 121,212) is always a multiple of 7.

26

Represent the six-digit number as ABABAB. Explain why Benjamin's discovery is correct by referring to Benjamin's previous notes in problem (A). (40 points)

$$\left[\right]$$

How to define a number that is multiple of 7

Let's show how to find out if a number is a multiple of 7 or not.

First, split a multi-digit number into 3-digit numbers starting from the ones place. For example, when a number 1,001,020,300 is given, you split the numbers like this: 1/001/020/300. From this process you have made the four numbers 1, 1, 20, and 300.

Second, find the sum of the numbers in the odd number places starting from the left. Then find the sum of the numbers in the even number places starting from the left. (For example, 1 (odd), 001 (even), 020 (odd), 300 (even))

　　The sum of the numbers in odd places: $1 + 20 = 21$
　　The sum of the numbers in even places: $1 + 300 = 301$

If the difference of these two sums is a multiple of 7 or a multiple of 0, the original number is a multiple of 7, also.

　　$301 - 21 = 280$
　　$280 \div 7 = 40$
　　So, 1,001,020,300 is a multiple of 7.

This method is incredible, because we can determine whether a given large number is a multiple of 7 or not without actually dividing the large number by 7.

1 Benjamin got really interested in finding a way to determine if a given number is a multiple of a specific number. So, he went to the library and found a math book that had the following information about how to determine if a given number is a multiple of a specific number.

> **To find if a given number is a multiple of a specific number we can use "divisibility rules."**
>
> - If the last digit is a multiple of 2 or 0, then the number is divisible by 2. (In other words, the number is a multiple of 2.)
> - If the last two digits are a number that is a multiple of 4 or 0, then the number is divisible by 4. (In other words, the number is a multiple of 4.)
> - If the last three digits are 000 or a number that is a multiple of 8, the number is divisible by 8. (In other words, the number is a multiple of 8.)
> - If the last four digits are 000 or a number that is a multiple of 16, the number is divisible by 16. (In other words, the number is a multiple of 16.)

Ⓐ Given the numbers below, find and list all numbers that are multiples of 4. (15 points)

| 24688642 | 46822864 |

| 68244286 | 82466428 |

( )

Ⓑ Fill in the box ☐ with a number from 0 to 9 to make an 8-digit number that is a multiple of 8. (15 points)

1234567 ☐

28

C There is a hidden rule among the divisibility rules shown to the left. Find the rule and explain why it is called "the divisibility rule of 64." (20 points)

2 Ms. Evans gave students a homework math challenge problem about divisibility (finding multiples). Benjamin is working on the problem about the divisibility rule of 11.

Challenge to become a math professor!

The divisibility rule of 11 (multiples of 11)

Starting from the left, find the sum of the numbers in odd places and the sum of the numbers in even places. If the difference between the two sums is 0 or is divisible by 11, the number is a multiple of 11.

A Is 18181818181818181 a multiple of 11? Please explain. (30 points)

B Think of a five-digit number that is composed of different numerals. What is the smallest multiple of 11? (20 points)

(   )

Hint

The smallest five-digit number that is composed of different numerals is 10234.
So, let's consider a multiple of 11 to be 102AB.

1 Olivia, Emma, Maia, Theo, and Liam are chocolate lovers. They are organizing a chocolate party to exchange their favorite chocolates. They are very excited and are thinking a lot about what kind of chocolate they will bring to their party.

Ⓐ Olivia decided to make her own chocolate. She melts chocolate bars and pours them into small aluminum molds. She used 3 chocolate bars of 40 grams each to make a total of 16 chocolate pieces. What is the average weight of a piece of her chocolate in grams?
(10 points for the math sentence, 10 points for the answer)

Math Sentence

Answer (   )

Ⓑ Olivia bought 10 heart-shaped, 3 star-shaped, and 7 circle-shaped aluminum molds when she was making the chocolates described in problem Ⓐ. The average price of an aluminum mold is 10.5 cents. How much did she pay to purchase all the aluminum molds? (10 points for the math sentence, 10 points for the answer)

Math Sentence

Answer (   )

C Emma went to Pop Chocolate Store to buy her chocolates. Pop Chocolate has 7 kinds of chocolate that are wrapped in individual pieces. A salesperson told her, "The average price of a piece of wrapped chocolate is 93 cents." Emma decided to buy one piece of each kind of chocolate. If she pays with a $10 bill, how much change will she get?
(15 points for the math sentence, 15 points for the answer)

Math Sentence

Answer ( )

D Maia found a chocolate store that sells chocolate by the weight. She can fill a plastic bag with up to 250 grams of chocolates.

She put 8 pieces of chocolate in a bag and measured the bag's weight. The weight was 25.6 g, so the average weight of a piece of chocolate is ① [ ] g. If she uses this average weight and continues to fill the bag until it has 30 chocolates, the total weight of the chocolate will be about ② [ ] g. Moreover, if the total weight of chocolate reaches 250 g, she will know there are about ③ [ ] pieces of chocolate in the bag.

Fill in the [ ] with appropriate numbers. In space ③, make sure your answer is expressed as a whole number by rounding at the first decimal place (rounding the tenths to a whole number). (10 points each)

31

14 The Mechanism of Averages (Part 2)

Date
. .

Score
/100

1 Olivia, Emma, Maia, Theo, and Liam are at the chocolate party and starting to exchange chocolates. Each friend brought chocolates in different numbers and a variety of sizes; however, the chocolates each friend brought are wrapped to look like gifts.

Theo and Liam said to the others, "Let's make some math problems about averages using our gifts of chocolate!" Theo and Liam started to find the weight and the number of chocolates in each gift.

Ⓐ Theo made a math problem as shown below. Let's solve this problem.
(20 points for the math sentence, 20 points for the answer)

Theo's Math Problem

The average weight of three gifts of chocolate prepared by Olivia, Emma, and Maia is 210 g. The average of two gifts of chocolate prepared by Liam and Theo is 295 g. What is the average weight of the five gifts?

Math Sentence

Answer ( )

Ⓑ Liam is making a math problem about averages also. He found the average number of chocolates in a gift was 27. Then, he thought about the following: "I put fewer chocolates in my gift than the average. If we compare everyone's number of chocolates, I wonder if the number of chocolates in my gift will fall within the lower end among all five gifts, also."

The numbers of Liam's friends' chocolates are shown in the table below.

	Olivia	Emma	Maia	Theo
Number of Chocolates	18	7	78	12

Fill in the [ ] below with appropriate numbers, fill in blank ③ with an ordinal number, and blank ④ with the word "higher" or "lower." (15 points each)

The total number of chocolates the five friends prepared is ① [ ]. The number of chocolates Liam prepared is ② [ ]. Liam's number of chocolate is the ③ [ ] greatest among the five sets of chocolates. When Liam compared his number of chocolates to the other four numbers, his number falls within the ④ [ ] lower range of the five numbers.

Median

When several values are ordered from the least to the greatest, the value located in the middle is called the **median**. (If there is an even number of values, the average of the two middle values is the median.)

For example, look at the numbers of chocolates prepared by the five people from the greatest to the least in Problem **B** above. Olivia's 18 chocolates are third in the ordered list, which is also the median value. When you want to know whether a given value falls within the higher or lower range, it is better to think about and refer to the median.

When you hear about or read test scores, often only the average score is reported. However, if you want to determine where your score stands among the test scores in a group or whether your score is higher or lower than most test scores in a group of scores, you should compare your score to the median value.

So, if you understand when and how to use the median, your math reasoning will be awesome and will help you understand even more about your performance in math!

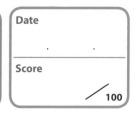

1 Benjamin visited his friend Yuki. She has four puppies and their names are Spring, Summer, Autumn, and Winter. Yuki told Benjamin the order of the birth of those four puppies, as follows: "Summer was born after the dog that was born after Spring. One dog was born before and one dog was born after Autumn. Winter was born after Spring."

In what birthplace order was Winter born? Explain your answer. (30 points)

(   )

2 Benjamin, Emilio, and Ryan are talking about dates that they can play together from the 1st to the 7th of a given month.

Benjamin: I have something to do on the 2nd and 4th.
Emilio: I'm not free on Monday, Tuesday, Friday and Saturday.
Benjamin: Emilio, you are not free on the days when I'm not free either.
Ryan: I'm available on even days. So, the day we all three can play together will be this day.

What date and day of the week is Ryan thinking of? (30 points)

(   )

3 Benjamin, Emilio and Ryan are playing cards. Emilio got the following 10 cards and put all of his cards down on the table so all can see them.

Suit	Hearts	Clubs	Spades	Diamond
Numbers	1, 3, 12	11, 13	1, 8, 11	8, 12

Emilio mentally chose one of the 10 cards on the table. Then he told only the card's suit (pictorial symbol) to Benjamin and only its number to Ryan.

Benjamin: I don't know which card Emilio chose in his head. You don't know the card, do you, Ryan?

Ryan: I didn't know at first, but I know the card now by listening what you said, Benjamin.

Benjamin: I see, if that is the case I know what it is!

Which card did Emilio choose? Write the suit (pictorial symbol) and the number.
(20 points each)

Suit ( )

Number ( )

If Emilio chooses the 3 or the 13 card, Ryan will know which card is the one Emilio's thinking of!

1 Benjamin went to the Park City shopping mall. The shops are running a quiz campaign and participants will have a chance to get special gifts or discount tickets. Benjamin went to as many shops as possible.

Ⓐ He found the quiz board below at Home Cooking Restaurant.

Free dessert offer: Home Cooking Restaurant

Abe, Brad, Carl, and David are brothers. They are lined up outside in alphabetical order waiting for the restaurant to open. They are talking about today's special offer.

- Brad : The restaurant offers customers one free dessert today.
- David : The brother who stands two places before me speaks the truth.
- Carl : The person standing in front of me is not telling the truth.
- Abe : The last brother in line tells the truth.

Among the four brothers, three tell the truth and one is lying. Does the restaurant offer a free dessert today?

Identify who is telling a lie. Describe if the Home Cooking Restaurant is giving a free dessert today. (20 points each)

Who is lying? ( )

Does the restaurant offer a free dessert today? ( )

B Then, Benjamin went to the Delicious Bakery. He found the quiz board below and bags that contain bagels. He can't see what kind of bagel is in each bag.

> ## Delicious Bakery's Quiz: What kind of bagels are in the bags?
>
> There are 3 bags on the table. Each bag contains one kind of bagel: onion, cinnamon raisin, or whole wheat. There is a card attached to each bag. The truth is written on the card that is attached to the bag that contains the onion bagel. The words written on the card attached to the bag that contains a cinnamon raisin is a lie. We don't know whether the card on the whole wheat bagel tells the truth or not.
>
> Card 1: This is not an onion bagel.
> Card 2: This is not a whole wheat bagel.
> Card 3: This is not a cinnamon raisin bagel.
>
> Can you tell what kind of bagel each bag contains? If you can solve it, you will get a discount ticket!

Benjamin wants to buy a whole wheat bagel. What card number should he choose?
(30 points)

(   )

C He found the quiz board below at a cheese shop.

> ## Which mouse ate the cheese?
>
> There were 5 mice and one of them ate the swiss cheese. The five mice are talking about who ate the swiss cheese. Three of them are telling the truth and the other two are lying.
>
> > Taffy: It's not Timmy who ate the swiss cheese.
> > Teddy: It is Toffee or Timmy.
> > Timmy: Teddy is lying.
> > Toby: Timmy ate the swiss cheese.
> > Toffee: Teddy and Toby are telling the truth.
>
> We will give a special gift of a very tasty new cheese to those people who identify which mouse ate the swiss cheese!

Which mouse ate the swiss cheese? (30 points)

(   )

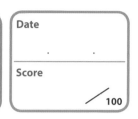

1 Emily is making cookies. Before baking the cookies, she will put them on a square cookie sheet (baking pan) with a side length of 31 cm. She wants to leave 1 cm of space from the edge of the tray and 1 cm between each cookie. In addition, she wants to make sure that the tray is filled with cookies and there is no extra unused space on the tray.

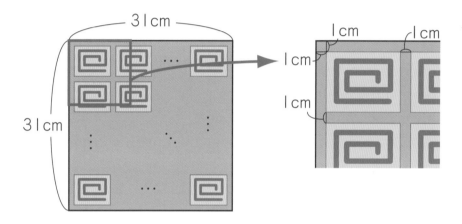

Ⓐ She arranged rectangular-shaped cookies on her tray. Each rectangular cookie has a length of 5 cm and a width of 4 cm. Emily placed each rectangular cookie in the same orientation as shown above. How many cookies was she able to place on her cookie sheet? (30 points)

( )

If you can solve this, the math - and you - are cool!

To solve this problem, you could count the space and the length of the cookies in order, such as "space, cookie, space, cookie, space, …" but if you can think of a better (more mathematical) way, that would be super. For example, let's think about the problem by combining a cookie and surrounding spaces … to make a set of shapes like the one below.

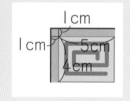

B When Emily arranged square-shaped cookies on a cookie sheet of the same size, she could bake a total of 36 cookies. Find the length of the sides of the square-shaped cookie. (30 points)

(   )

C Then, Emily is thinking about putting square cookies on a cookie sheet that is 29 cm long and 9 cm wide. She left 1 cm spaces from the edges of the tray to the cookie as before. She would like to place as many same-size square cookies of the largest size possible. Find the length of a side of these square-shaped cookies. (40 points)

(   )

18 Let's Use Factors! (Part 2)

1 Emily is packaging cookies into gift bags to give to her friends.

A She wants to put 35 cookies into each gift bag. If she puts the same number of cookies into bags without any cookies left over, how many bags could she make? Record all possible cases, including the case of her putting all cookies into one bag. (20 points)

(   )

B She decided to put some cookies and candies into gift bags. She wants to make sure she makes 3 or more bags. Each bag must have an equal number of cookies and candies inside without having any leftovers. She has 35 cookies and 15 candies. How many bags can she make? (30 points)

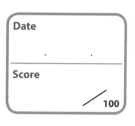

(   )

C Now, Emily decided to put some cookies and gumballs into gift bags. She has 28 cookies and 21 gumballs. First of all, she put the same number of cookies into each bag, and as a result, 4 cookies left over. After that, she also put the same number of gumballs into the same bag that she put the cookies in order to make them wrapped together, and then 5 gumballs left over. She would like to put as many bags as possible. How many bags did she make? (50 points)

(   )

👑
✨ If you can solve this, the math - and you - are cool! ✨

Let's think about Problem C by first considering the number of cookies and gumballs after subtracting those that were left over. Then pay attention to the number of remaining cookies and gumballs compared to the number of cookies and gumballs in the bags.

Date

Score
/ 100

1 A Westside Elementary School festival will be held soon. The Westside fourth and fifth grade students will prepare activities and invite Kindergarten to third grade students. Harvey and his Grade 5 Class 1 classmates are discussing the activities, but they are having difficulty agreeing on what activities they would like to offer and prepare.

Ⓐ The list of nominated activities is shown below. Activities are split into three categories: games, arts and crafts, and explorations.

Games: bowling, basketball shots, ring toss, fishing, treasure hunt
Arts & Crafts: wind chimes, origami, sailboats, T-shirt dyeing
Explorations: ghost house, maze

Each of 33 classmates in the Grade 5 Class 1 will write one of the three categories on a piece of paper and cast a vote. A category will be decided by the majority. Tatiana is hoping that the class chooses the Games category. For the Games category to be chosen without fail, at least how many votes does Games need to get? (30 points)

(   )

Hint

Think about the situation where the number of votes cast for Games is so high that the Games category is chosen.

B) The Games category was chosen, as Tatiana had hoped. Now the class is going to choose three games out of the five games nominated. Each of 33 classmates will write only one of the five games on a piece of paper and cast a vote. The three highest-voted games will be chosen. Tatiana wants to play the ring toss game at the festival.

① In order for ring toss to be chosen without fail, at least how many votes does ring toss need to get? (30 points)

(   )

② The students have completed the voting process. Ms. Grant, the teacher, announces the voting results starting with the games that got the highest number of votes. First place is "basketball shots," which has 10 votes; and second place is "bowling," which has 8 votes. If third place is "ring toss," fourth place is "fishing," and last place is "treasure hunt," what are all possible combinations of voting numbers for third through fifth place that could give these results? Write these combinations in the table below.
(Note: You may not need all the rows to answer this question.) (40 points)

Possible Number of Votes

Ring Toss	Fishing	Treasure Hunt

Let's Take a Vote (Part 2)

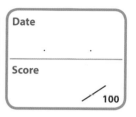

1 Westside Elementary School's festival has finished. All 525 students from kindergarten to third grade are voting for their favorite grade's activities. Each student will vote twice and follow the rules given below.

> **Voting Rules:**
> All kindergarten to 3rd grade students will vote twice
> One vote to choose the favorite class among the 5th grade classes
> One vote to choose the favorite class among the 4th grade classes

The class that has the most votes among three 5th grade classes and among four 4th grade classes will receive awards from the Westside principal at the next school assembly.

The voting period finally comes to an end, and the votes are being counted.

Ⓐ The interim report shows the number of votes for each 5th grade class.

Grade 5	Class 1	Class 2	Class 3
Number of votes	86	191	142

① In order for Class 2 to get first place without fail, at least how many votes does Class 2 need to get? (30 points)

(   )

② Is it possible for Class 1 to get first place? Please answer "yes" or "no," and explain
   your reasoning. (30 points)

B The interim report shows the number of votes for each 4th grade class.

Grade 4	Class 1	Class 2	Class 3	Class 4
Number of votes	89	45	138	162

Is it possible for Class 2 to get first or second place? Explain your answer and reasoning.
(40 points)

It's awesome if you know!

Grade 5 Class 4 will be awarded without fail

At this point it has already been decided that Class 4 will be awarded the first or
second place without fail.

You can verify this using the numbers of the vote shown in the interim report
above. Think about it!

(Check this solution in the "Answers & Explanations" section of the book.)

1 Look at the arrangement of matchsticks.

Alex and Benjamin found the number of matchsticks by setting up math sentences.

Alex

$1 + 3 \times 8 = 25$ (matchsticks)

Benjamin

$4 + 3 \times (8 - 1) = 25$ (matchsticks)

Interpret Alex and Benjamin's math sentences to explain how they solved the problem. (20 points eatch)

Alex

Benjamin

2 Look at the picture of green counters. Maritza, Elle, and Mario found the number of counters by using the math sentences below. Use the figures and explain in writing how each student solved to find the number of counters. (20 points eatch)

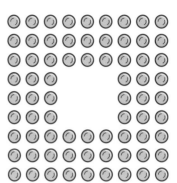

A Maritza

$3 \times 3 \times 8 = 72$ (counters)

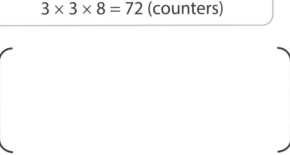

B Elle

$9 \times 9 - 3 \times 3 = 72$ (counters)

C Mario

$6 \times 3 \times 4 = 72$ (counters)

22 Ideas for Calculating Easily and Accurately (Part 1)

Date . .

Score /100

1 Properties of operations can be used to calculate easily and accurately. Oscar wants to be better at calculations, so he is trying to solve calculation problems using properties of operations. Accurately calculate problems 1 to 3 by using the properties of operations shown below and any other properties of operations you have previously learned. (20 points eatch)

Properties of Operations:

$$A \times B + A \times C + A \times D = A\,(B + C + D)$$
$$A \times B - A \times C + A \times D = A\,(B - C + D)$$

Ⓐ $3.14 \times 14 + 39 \times 3.14 + 3.14 \times 47$

Ⓑ $\frac{6}{7} \times 43 - \frac{3}{7} \times 45 + \frac{9}{7} \times 12$

Ⓒ $7 \times 1.1 \times 9.5 + 9.5 \times 7 \times 3.4 + 5.5 \times 9.5 \times 7$

Hint

In problems Ⓑ and Ⓒ, we can't immediately use the properties of operations listed above. So, let's think about how we can find "A" in the Properties of Operations listed above.

2 Oscar and Violet are discussing the ideas to solve a problem that involves multiplication of decimals.

Oscar: We had a lot of homework on multiplication of decimals. I solved the problems using an algorithm and paying attention to the locations of decimal points.

Violet: It's easy to make mistakes when multiplying decimals. Actually, when I did my homework, I did some calculations mentally, such as 2.3×10.1.

Oscar: Wow! How did you do that? Could you tell me how to do it?

Violet: I split 10.1 into 10 and 0.1. If you do that, then the calculation can be done mentally because multiplying by 10 or 0.1 is easy.

Oscar: I see! I'll try to use your strategy and do the calculations.

Ⓐ Solve 2.3×10.1 mentally. (20 points)

(   )

Ⓑ Referring to Violet's calculation strategy, solve 3.5×9.9 mentally. (20 points)

(   )

It will be awesome, if you can calculate decimals mentally!

1 Mr. Ellington, a 5th grade teacher, gave Nathan and Molly a math problem.

Problem:

Numbers A and B are whole numbers. Find all pairs of numbers that can be substitutes for A and B in the math sentence below.

$A \times B - A = 5$

Mr. Ellington, Nathan, and Molly are discussing the solution.

Nathan:　　　There are two unknown numbers in the math sentence.

Molly:　　　Yes. A is a whole number, so …

　　　　　　When A is 1, then what is B? I wonder if B is a whole number …

　　　　　　When A is 2, then what is B? I wonder if B is a whole number …

　　　　　　I tried to find the numbers by thinking like that, but there are so many whole numbers! So, I thought this way of thinking is too complicated.

Nathan:　　　Yes, it is difficult. I wonder if there is another way to solve this problem. Mr. Ellington, would you please give us a hint?

Mr. Ellington: Let's look at the math sentence carefully. You have two A's on the left side of the equal sign. Using one of the properties of operations, can you think of a way to transform the sentence?

Nathan:　　　Well, if I apply the properties of sentences to $A \times B - A$, it will be a product of two numbers. So the product is 5 … I think now I will be able to find the answer.

Molly:　　　I think I can find the answer, too. I will try to solve it.

Refer to the dialogue between the teacher and the two students above. Find all pairs of numbers A and B that can be written as (A, B). (30 points.)

(　　　　　　　　　　　)

2 Find all whole numbers that can replace B in the sentence below. (30 points)

B × B – B = 12

(   )

3 Numbers A and B are whole numbers. Find all pairs of numbers that can be substituted for A and B that can be written as (A, B).

A × B – A + B – 1 = 2

A The math sentence A × B – A + B – 1 can be transformed into

(A + [①   ]) (B – [②   ]).

Fill in the blanks in the math sentence above with appropriate numbers.
(10 points each)

If you can solve this, the math – and you – are cool!

Try using the properties of operations by paying attention to A × B – A.

B Referring to problem **A** above, find all pairs of numbers A and B that can be written as (A, B). (20 points)

(   )

1 Maria and her family have been saving one-cent coins in a piggy bank since October. She wants to save 10,000 coins to give a present to her grandparents.

The table below shows the number of coins they saved from October through January.

October	November	December	January
2,953	1,849	1,509	2,819

Maria and her brother use approximate numbers to check how many coins are in the piggy bank.

A Maria rounded each month's number to the nearest thousand before adding to find the sum. She found the total number of coins was less than 10,000. Explain why. (30 points)

B Maria's brother rounded numbers to the nearest hundred before adding to find the sum. He found they needed 1,000 more coins to achieve 10,000. Explain why. (30 points)

2 Ms. Nelson created a challenging math problem about approximate numbers. She hopes her students can meet the challenge by showing they have strong mathematics problem solving skills.

(A) The numbers 12,345 and 6,789 were added to a whole number. When the sum was rounded, the result was an approximate number of 12,300. What is the smallest possible number for the whole number that was added? (20 points)

(   )

(B) A whole number is divided by 12. When the quotient is rounded at the tenth place, the quotient becomes 34. If you add all the whole numbers that satisfy this condition, what will be the total? (20 points)

(   )

1 A barcode is a series of vertical lines printed on a product. Bar codes provide a method to track and store information about products. Barcodes make doing business much more efficient for companies and reduces the number of human errors. When we buy products at a store, barcodes are scanned by a barcode reader. The international barcode uses 13 digits to represents four categories of data: country of origin, company's name, product's name, and barcode scan checking number. The country codes of USA and Canada are 00 through 13. The country codes of Japan are 45 and 49. Using the barcode data, companies are able to know what products are purchased, stored, or sold.

The barcode scanner is used to read the barcodes, but if the scanner cannot read the barcode correctly it causes a big problem. So, in order to avoid errors, a "check digit" is used as the last digit. The check digit is assigned with the following rules using the first 12 digits of numbers:

A. Starting from the left, find the sum of all odd position numbers.

B. Find the sum of even position numbers starting from the left again, then multiply the sum by 3.

C. Find the sum of A and B above.

D. Find the nearest multiple of 10 that is greater than or equal to the number you found in C, then find the difference between that number and the number you found in C. The difference is used as the "Check code number."

Fill in the ☐s to complete the 13-digit barcodes below. (20 points each)

Ⓐ 491357902468 ☐

Ⓑ 45158 ☐ 2603714

2 Karen, Megan, Amy, and Kimberly took a challenging test. They are talking about their test results.

Karen: The average score for the four of us is 86 points.
Megan: My score is 6 points lower than Karen's score.
Amy: My score is 12 points higher than Karen's score.
Kimberly: My score is 8 points higher than the average of your three scores.

Find Karen's test score. (20 points)

(   )

3 There are 5 identical bags. Each bag contains some coins. Three of the bags are filled with real coins and 2 of them are filled with fake coins. One real coin weighs 10 grams and one fake coin weighs 9 grams.

There is a way to use the scale only one time to identify which bags hold real coins and which bags hold fake coins. Take out some coins from any of the bags and find the total weight of these coins using a scale only once. Explain how you can do this by taking out a minimum number of coins from the bags. (40 points)

(   )

If you can solve this, the math - and you - are cool!

This is a very difficult problem!
First label the bags, A, B, C, D, and E.
For example, let's say we take out one coin from each bag. Then we use the scale one time to find the total weight of those five coins. Regardless of which two bags hold fake coins (A and B or C and D, etc.), the total weight will be the same (e.g., 9 + 9 + 10 + 10 + 10 = 48 g).

Therefore, it is important to vary the number of coins you take out from the bags. It is important also to think about different combinations of the number of coins that could be taken from each bag as a way to determine which two bags hold fake coins and how the total weight would vary. Make an organized list and think logically.

26 Addition and Subtraction of Decimals

Date

Score

/100

1 Calculate the following. (6 points each)

(A) $0.5 + 0.07 + 1.28$

(B) $3.54 + 4.78 + 6.89$

(C) $8.8 - 2.45 - 1.07$

(D) $12.5 - 0.48 - 5.86$

(E) $8.25 - 2.58 + 3.69$

(F) $15.39 - (5.76 + 7.24)$

Think about a better way to calculate the following. (8 points each)

(A) $4.35 + 3.43 + 5.57$

(B) $7.72 + 5.45 + 6.28$

2 Think about a better way to calculate the following.   (8 points each)

Ⓐ 0.01 + 0.02 + 0.03 + 0.04 + 0.05 + 0.06 + 0.07 + 0.08 + 0.09 + 0.1

Ⓑ 0.1−0.09 + 0.08−0.07 + 0.06−0.05 + 0.04−0.03 + 0.02−0.01

3 Put appropriate addition or subtraction (+ or −) signs in the ☐s below to make the sentences true.   (10 points for each problem)

Ⓐ 2.45 ☐ 0.39 ☐ 3.25 = 6.09

Ⓑ 6.57 ☐ 0.88 ☐ 2.76 = 8.45

> Think about each problem systematically; for example, you could first try addition to see what the second operation should be to give you the answer.

1 Jada is talking about the relationship between fractions and decimal numbers with her friends.

Jada: We can convert a fraction into a decimal number by using division.
          For example : $\frac{1}{2} = 1 \div 2 = 0.5$

Emma: That's right. If we calculate $1 \div 7$, it is $0.142857\ldots$ It looks like it's indivisible. Can't we write $\frac{1}{7}$ as an exact decimal number?

Noel: My grandfather said that there are two types of fractions: one type can be converted to decimal numbers and the other type cannot be converted to decimal numbers. He told me if we continue to calculate $1 \div 7$, we can find a pattern of numbers after the decimal point. Jada and Emma, can you find the pattern?

Ⓐ When the fraction $\frac{1}{7}$ is converted to a decimal number, what number will be in the seventh decimal place? (20 points)

(   )

Ⓑ Explain the number pattern mentioned by Noel. Then, find the number in the seventy-seventh decimal place? (15 points each)

The number pattern

$\Bigg[$ 　　　　　　　　　　　　　　 $\Bigg]$

The number in the seventy-seventh decimal place (   )

58

2 Mr. Grant is sharing with Jada and her friends an interesting result of multiplying decimal numbers using the number pattern 142857 that was obtained after converting $\frac{1}{7}$ into a decimal number.

Try calculating the multiplication of decimal numbers Ⓐ through Ⓔ below.
As you calculate, numbers in the product will form a pattern as indicated in the diagram below. Don't you think this is interesting?

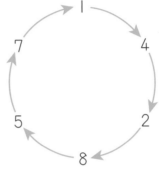

Calculate and verify what Mr. Grant told his students. (10 points each)

Ⓐ 1.42857×2

Ⓑ 1.42857×3

Ⓒ 1.42857×4

Ⓓ 1.42857×5

Ⓔ 1.42857×6

What do you think the result of the calculation 1.42857×7 will be?
Try the calculation. You will see an interesting answer.

Multiplication of Decimals (Part 1)

Date

Score

/100

1 Calculate the following. (8 points each)

A
```
    4.8
×     9
```

B
```
    5.8
×  8 0
```

C
```
    3.5
×  3 6
```

D
```
   4 3.2
×    6 5
```

E
```
   8.6 2
×      7
```

F
```
   5.6 3
×     4 0
```

G
```
   3.0 5
×  3 4 8
```

H
```
   0.3 7 6
×       2 4
```

2 Calculate the following. (7 points each)

Ⓐ $4.5 \times 2.4 + 5.5 \times 2.4$

Ⓑ $8.9 \times 35 - 8.9 \times 33$

Ⓒ $2.31 \times 50 + 23.1 \times 3 + 231 \times 0.2$

Ⓓ $3.8 \times 5 + 7.6 \times 8$

When we calculate Ⓓ above, I wonder if we could use $3.8 \times 2 = 7.6$ to make the calculation easier.

3 There are many marbles in a bag. The weight of each marble is more than 2.5 g and less than 3.5 g. If you pick six marbles from the bag and measure the total weight, what could be the weight of the six marbles? Please state your answer for the total weight as more than ___ grams and less than ___ grams. (8 points)

(more than ___ g and less than ___ g)

29 Multiplication of Decimals (Part 2)

Date

Score /100

1 Use algorithms to calculate the following problems. (5 points each)

Ⓐ 30×0.2

Ⓑ 43×1.7

Ⓒ 27×9.8

Ⓓ 121×0.55

Ⓔ 7.3×9.6

Ⓕ 4.1×0.75

Ⓖ 3.14×6.2

Ⓗ 4.34×7.05

Ⓘ 9.16×2.87

2 Use the calculation $123 \times 45 = 5535$ to find the products of the following problems.
(5 points each)

Ⓐ 12.3×4.5

Ⓑ 1230×0.45

Ⓒ 0.123×45000

3 Think about and apply an efficient strategy to calculate the following problems.
(20 points each)

Ⓐ $3.14 \times 4.8 + 3.14 \times 5.2$

Ⓑ $4 \times 7.23 \times 25$

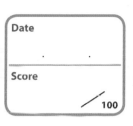

Date

Score

/ 100

1 Fill in the ☐s below with the appropriate inequality symbol (>, <) that represents the relationship between products and factors. (10 points each)

Ⓐ 6×0.7 ☐ 6

Ⓑ 230×1.01 ☐ 230

Ⓒ 3.14×1.9 ☐ 3.14

Ⓓ 2.73×0.98 ☐ 2.73

2 How many cm² is the sum of the area of rectangles A, B and C? (15 points each)

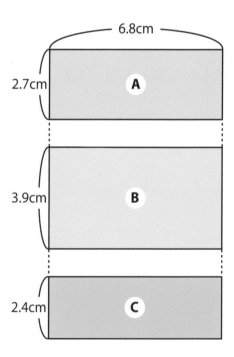

(　　　　　　　)

3 Solve the following problems (15 points each)

A There are 15 fish tanks. Each tank holds 5.2 gallons of water. How many gallons of water will it take to fill all 15 fish tanks?

( )

B A car can travel 13.8 km (kilometers) on 1 L (liter) of fuel. If the car has 5.6L of fuel in its tank, how many km can the car travel before it runs out of gas?

( )

C You are driving the car discussed in problem **B**. The car had 4.3 L of fuel in the tank before you left home. After you drove a few hours you noticed the fuel was low, so you added 7.5 L of fuel at a gas station. When you arrived back home there was 2 L of fuel left in the tank. How many km had your car traveled?

( )

If you can solve this, the math - and you - are cool!

Let's think about how many liters of fuel you used in total, between departure and arrival?

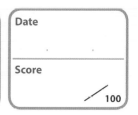

Date

Score

⁄ 100

1 Calculate the following. (10 points each)

A

$8\overline{)54.4}$

B

$34\overline{)91.8}$

C

$48\overline{)34.2}$

D

$9\overline{)23.04}$

E

$17\overline{)9.52}$

F

$7\overline{)0.175}$

2 Divide completely the following. (10 points each)

A

$$5\overline{)4.3}$$

B

$$8\overline{)100}$$

C

$$25\overline{)121}$$

3 A number was to be divided by 8, but it was mistakenly multiplied by 8 and the product became 31.2. Correct the mistake and show the correct calculation. If you need to divide, please divide completely. (10 points)

$$(\qquad\qquad)$$

We need to find the unknown starting number first.

Division of Decimals (Part 2)

1 Calculate the following and show the quotient to one decimal place (tenths) and the remainder. (15 points each)

Ⓐ 38.9÷7

Ⓑ 42.5÷9

2 Answer to the following questions. (15 points each)

Ⓐ Calculate 128 ÷ 47 and find the quotient by rounding it to the highest 2 places.

(   )

Ⓑ Calculate 974 ÷ 38 and find the quotient by rounding it to the first decimal place (tenths).

(   )

3 There is a flower bed with an area of 32.5 m². If the width of the flower bed is 2 m, what is its length? (20 points)

(   )

4 The length of a blue ribbon is 46 cm and the length of a yellow ribbon is 115 cm. How many times longer is the length of the yellow ribbon than the blue ribbon? (20 points)

> To find how many times as much/as many as one is to other, it is a good idea to represent the number that we are looking for with a ☐ and construct an sentence.

(   )

It's awesome if you know!

The size of per unit quantity to compare

Units such as "area per person" and "price per 1 m" are called "per unit" quantities. By finding a per unit quantity you can compare quantities such as how crowded different rooms are.

(Example)

Using the weight of wire per meter, compare the weight of two wires A and B that weigh 200 g for 4 m and 245 g for 5 meters:

Wire A: $200 \div 4 = 50$ (g)
Wire B: $245 \div 5 = 49$ (g)

By comparing the weight per 1 m, we can tell that wire A is heavier than wire B.

Date

Score

/100

1 Shaquille found the following rule for calculating fractions:

> The size of a fraction does not change if you multiply or divide the denominator and the numerator by the same number

For example, when the denominator and numerator of the fraction $\frac{1}{2}$ is multiplied by 6,729, it will be $\frac{1}{2} = \frac{6729}{13458}$.

Shaquille is challenging himself to solve a fraction puzzle that uses this rule.

⭐ **Fraction Puzzle**

The fraction $\frac{6729}{13458}$ uses all numbers from 1 to 9 once. Among fractions that use numbers 1 to 9 only once, such as $\frac{6729}{13458}$, there are only 12 fractions that equal $\frac{1}{2}$. Among these fractions, three of them have 9 in the thousands place of the numerator. Find these three fractions.

Find the answer to the fraction puzzle. (20 points each)

(   ) (   ) (   )

You might want to think about the ten-thousands place of the denominator and the one-thousands place of the numerator, first.

70

2 Pizzeria Cucina is famous for delicious pizzas. The restaurant gives points when customers purchase food. The customers save points and use them to get free pizzas. Today is February 9th and it is National Pizza Day. The picture below shows Pizzeria Cucina's National Pizza Day special instructions about how to use the points accumulated by a customer. Unfortunatelly, the points customers need to get a free $\frac{1}{4}$ of a regular size pizza were erased accidently by someone at the shop.

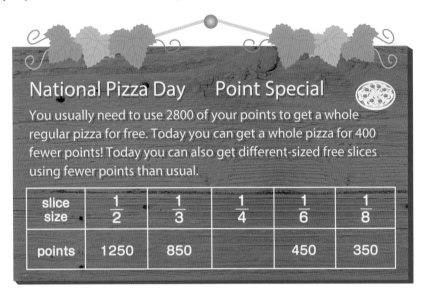

National Pizza Day — Point Special

You usually need to use 2800 of your points to get a whole regular pizza for free. Today you can get a whole pizza for 400 fewer points! Today you can also get different-sized free slices using fewer points than usual.

slice size	$\frac{1}{2}$	$\frac{1}{3}$	$\frac{1}{4}$	$\frac{1}{6}$	$\frac{1}{8}$
points	1250	850		450	350

The restaurant owner uses a rule for the points needed to get different-sized free slices. To figure out the rule, look at the table the restaurant owner posted. Then, find the points needed to get $\frac{1}{4}$ of a regular size pizza free.

Math Sentence

Answer $\Big($ $\Big)$

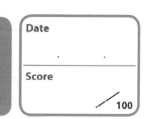

1 Shaquille is interested in calculating fraction numbers. He went to the school library to find out more about fraction calculations. In one of the books he found, there was a fraction sentence as shown here. He didn't understand why this sentence was correct, because he had not yet learned about adding and subtracting fractions with different denominators at school. So, he tried to learn more about fraction calculations from the book.

$$\frac{1}{2} - \frac{1}{3} = \frac{1}{6}$$

A Using a rectangular model split into 6 equal parts (sixths), as shown here, helps us to understand why the sentence $\frac{1}{2} - \frac{1}{3} = \frac{1}{6}$ is correct. When the whole rectangle is shaded, it represents 1 whole. Shade the blocks below and verify that the sentence $\frac{1}{2} - \frac{1}{3} = \frac{1}{6}$ is correct. (20 points)

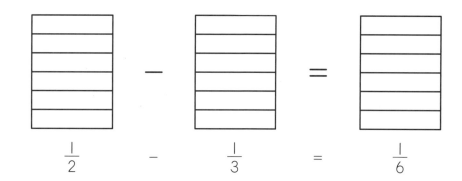

$$\frac{1}{2} \qquad - \qquad \frac{1}{3} \qquad = \qquad \frac{1}{6}$$

B Using a rectangular model split into 12 equal parts (twelfths), Shaquille understood that the sentence $\frac{1}{3} - \frac{1}{4} = \frac{1}{12}$ is correct. By studying the calculation, he discovered that he could solve $\frac{1}{4} - \frac{1}{5}$ without using a rectangular model. Shaquille said "It is important to pay attention to the denominators." What is the solution (answer) to the calculation so $\frac{1}{4} - \frac{1}{5}$? (20 points)

(   )

C Use the ideas learned from the previous problems 1 and 2 to calculate the following problems. (20 points each)

① $\dfrac{1}{2} + \dfrac{1}{6} + \dfrac{1}{12} + \dfrac{1}{20}$

 ② $\dfrac{1}{2} + \dfrac{1}{6} + \dfrac{1}{12} + \dfrac{1}{20} + \dfrac{1}{30} + \dfrac{1}{42} + \dfrac{1}{56} + \dfrac{1}{72} + \dfrac{1}{90}$

> $2 = 1 \times 2,\ 6 = 2 \times 3,\ 12 = 3 \times 4,\ 20 = 4 \times 5,\ \ldots\ldots$
> You might be able to find a better way to calculate!

D The next problem is a challenge problem. So, carefully solve it. (20 points)

⭐ Challenge Problem

$\bigcirc$ and $\triangle$ are whole numbers that are greater than 0 (zero). The sentence below is always satisfied when $\bigcirc$ and $\triangle$ are substituted with any whole numbers.

$$\dfrac{\bigcirc}{\triangle \times (\triangle + \bigcirc)} = \dfrac{1}{\triangle} - \dfrac{1}{\triangle + \bigcirc}$$

Calculate the following using the sentence above.

$$\dfrac{2}{3} + \dfrac{4}{21} + \dfrac{6}{91} = ?$$

(   )

1 Jonathan's grandfather told him an old tale about fractions.

Grandfather: A fraction whose numerator is 1, such as $\frac{1}{2}$ and $\frac{1}{3}$, is called a "unit fraction." When we add and subtract fractions, we used unit fractions as a base to think about calculating them. For example, we can think about how many one-tenths $\left(\frac{1}{10}\right)$ are in the fractions when adding $\frac{3}{10}$ and $\frac{5}{10}$.

Jonathan: I see. We call the amount of the base the "unit," so any fraction with a one (1) in the numerator is called a unit fraction, isn't it?

Grandfather: Exactly. I know an interesting story about unit fractions.

Jonathan: What kind of story is that? Please tell me!

Grandfather: A long time ago, Egyptians in Africa invented the concept of fractions. At that time, only the unit fractions were considered fractions.

Jonathan: How could the Egyptians have represented fractions with numerators more than or equal to 2?

Grandfather: Well, any fraction can be expressed as the sum of different unit fractions. Let's think about how we can represent both $\frac{2}{5}$ and $\frac{2}{11}$ as sums of different unit fractions. For example, $\frac{2}{5}$ can be represented as the sum of two unit fractions. First, identify the largest unit fraction that does not exceed $\frac{2}{5}$. Then find the other unit fraction that completes the sum of $\frac{2}{5}$. Repeat this process to find the sum of different unit fractions that equal $\frac{2}{11}$.

Jonathan: OK! I'll do my best!

Ⓐ Please fill in the ☐ with appropriate math sentences. (25 points each)

$$\frac{2}{5} = \boxed{}^①$$

$$\frac{2}{11} = \boxed{}^②$$

B Jonathan's grandfather gave him a note with a summary of the method for representing a fraction as the sum of unit fractions.

How to represent a fraction as the sum of unit fractions

❶ Divide the denominator by its numerator to find a whole number quotient.

❷ Add ❶ to the whole number quotient and use it as the denominator to make a unit fraction.

❸ Subtract the unit fraction from the original fraction.

❹ If the difference of the calculation is not a unit fraction, use the fraction to repeat steps ❶ through ❸ until you get a unit fraction.

❺ When the process of steps ❶ through ❸ produce a unit fraction, the calculation process will end. Then, add all the unit fractions you obtained. The answer should be equal to the original fraction.

Today is the 23rd of September and the autumnal equinox. Following the note he got from his grandfather, Jonathan decided to represent $\frac{9}{23}$ with a sum of different unit fractions. Let's solve the problem and write the math sentence in the [ ].
(50 points)

$$\frac{9}{23} = \boxed{}$$

How to express a fraction as the sum of unit fractions

There is another method to express a fraction as the sum of unit fractions. The point is to find the factors of the denominator that when added together equal the denominator. For example, let's think about the case of $\frac{13}{18}$. The factors of 18 are 1, 2, 3, 6, 9, 18. So if you select 1, 3, and 9 from the factors, the denominator 18 can be represented as $18 = 1 + 3 + 9$.

So, $\frac{13}{18}$ can be represented by the sum of unit fractions as:

$$\frac{13}{18} = \frac{1+3+9}{18} = \frac{1}{18} + \frac{3}{18} + \frac{9}{18} = \frac{1}{2} + \frac{1}{6} + \frac{1}{18}$$

36 Addition and Subtraction of Fractions (Part 1)

Date

Score /100

1 Convert the decimal to a fraction and the fraction to a decimal. (10 points each)

A 2.7

B $1\frac{3}{8}$

( )

( )

2 Calculate the following. (10 points each)

A $\frac{3}{4} + 1\frac{1}{3}$

B $5\frac{1}{6} - 3\frac{8}{9}$

( )

( )

C $1\frac{2}{3} + 2.25 - 3\frac{1}{12}$

D $3.6 - 1\frac{1}{8} + 3\frac{21}{40}$

( )

( )

3 Order the numbers in the () from the least to the greatest. (10 points each)

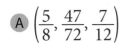 $\left(\dfrac{5}{8}, \dfrac{47}{72}, \dfrac{7}{12}\right)$

$($ →   → $)$

B $\left(1.25, \dfrac{11}{8}, \dfrac{27}{20}\right)$

$($ →   → $)$

4 Answer the questions below by considering only fractions that are greater than $\dfrac{2}{9}$ and less than $\dfrac{2}{7}$ and with denominators of 63. (10 points each)

A Find all fractions that satisfy the conditions as stated above.

$($ $)$

B Find all fractions that meet the conditions and that cannot be simplified.

$($ $)$

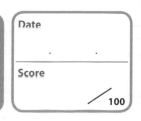

Date

Score

/100

1 Bottle A contains $1\frac{1}{4}$ L of milk and the bottle B contains $1\frac{2}{3}$ L of milk. How many L of milk are there altogether? (15 points)

$$\Big(\qquad\qquad\Big)$$

2 The distance between Maria's house and Kate's house is $1\frac{11}{18}$ km. The distance between Kate's house and Nina's house is $3\frac{7}{12}$ km. The distance between Nina's house and Anne's house is $5\frac{1}{6}$ km. Nina is thinking about going to Maria's house or Anne's house. Which distance is longer and how many km farther is the distance for Nina to walk? (25 points)

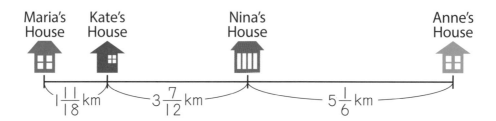

$$\Big(\text{The distance to }\qquad\text{'s house is }\qquad\text{ km farther.}\Big)$$

3 Takashi and Sam have color tapes. Takashi's tape is $\frac{1}{8}$ m longer than Sam's tape. When the two tapes are put together the length is $1\frac{1}{4}$ m. Please answer the following questions.

A We can draw a diagram as shown below to think about the problem. Write appropriate numbers in the [   ]s. (15 points each)

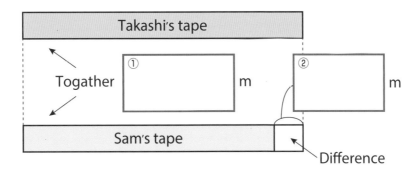

B What are the lengths of Takashi's tape and Sam's tape in m? (15 points each)

Takashi's tape ( )

Sam's tape ( )

Multiplication and Division of Fractions (Part 1)

Date . .

Score

/ 100

1 Calculate the following. (10 points each)

Ⓐ $\dfrac{2}{7} \times 5$

Ⓑ $\dfrac{7}{15} \times 18$

( )

( )

Ⓒ $\dfrac{5}{12} \times 8$

Ⓓ $\dfrac{4}{5} \div 7$

( )

( )

Ⓔ $\dfrac{8}{7} \div 4$

Ⓕ $\dfrac{15}{4} \div 6$

( )

( )

Problems Ⓐ to Ⓒ show fractions multiplied by whole numbers.
Problems Ⓓ to Ⓕ show fractions divided by whole numbers.

2 Calculate the following. (10 points each)

Ⓐ $3\frac{3}{5} \times 3 \div 6$

Ⓑ $\frac{12}{19} \div 2 \div 8$

( ) ( )

3 There is a square that has a perimeter of $\frac{14}{5}$ m. Answer the following questions. (10 points each)

Ⓐ How many meter is a side of this square?

( )

Ⓑ We are going to make an equilateral triangle whose side is $\frac{1}{45}$ m longer than a side of the square. What is the perimeter of this equilateral triangle?

( )

39 Multiplication and Division of Fractions (Part 2)

Date

Score

/100

1 Write appropriate fractions in the □s. (15 points each)

Ⓐ □ $\times 6 = 5\frac{1}{2}$

Ⓑ □ $\div 4 = 1\frac{1}{18}$

2 There are 8 plastic water bottles that weigh $4\frac{2}{7}$ kg in total. Please answer the following questions. (15 points each)

Ⓐ What is the weight of one plastic water bottle?

( )

Ⓑ What is the total weight of 21 plastic water bottles?

( )

3 A container has $\frac{2}{5}$ L of water. We are going to add $\frac{4}{15}$ L of water to this container every day. Please answer the following questions. (20 points each)

Amount of Water in the Container	
1st day	$\frac{2}{5}$ L
2nd day	$\left(\frac{2}{5} + \frac{4}{15}\right)$ L
3rd day	$\left(\frac{2}{5} + \frac{4}{15} + \frac{4}{15}\right)$ L
⋮	

Ⓐ How much water will be in the container on the 4th day?

(   )

Ⓑ How much water will be in the container on the 10th day?

(   )

👑 **If you can solve this, the math - and you - are cool!**

Think about how many $\frac{4}{15}$ L of water was added through the 10th day.

Multiplication and Division of Fractions (Part 3)

Date

Score

/ 100

1 Calculate the following. (10 points each)

Ⓐ $2\frac{6}{13} \div 2 - \frac{25}{26}$

( )

Ⓑ $\frac{3}{5} + \frac{2}{7} \times 2$

( )

Ⓒ $\frac{5}{9} + \frac{1}{6} \times 4 - \frac{8}{15} \div 6$

( )

Ⓓ $3\frac{1}{6} - 2\frac{2}{7} \div 8 + 1\frac{9}{14} \times 7 - \frac{8}{21}$

( )

2 Calculate the following. (15 points each)

Ⓐ $\dfrac{3}{4} - \left(\dfrac{4}{9} - \dfrac{5}{12} \right)$

( )

Ⓑ $\dfrac{8}{17} \div \left(6\dfrac{1}{4} - \dfrac{1}{24} \times 6 \right)$

( )

Ⓒ $2 - \left(4\dfrac{2}{5} \div 6 - \dfrac{7}{20} \right) \times 5$

( )

3 Write appropriate number in the space ☐ below. (15 points)

$$\left(\dfrac{4}{7} + \boxed{} \times 2 \right) \div 8 = \dfrac{6}{35}$$

👑
✦ If you can solve this, the math - and you - are cool! ✦

After finding the number that goes inside the ☐, make sure to check if the math sentence is correct by inserting the number and calculating to see if it equals $\dfrac{6}{35}$.

41 Multiplication of Fractions (Part 1)

Date

Score /100

1 Calculate the following. (5 points eatch)

Ⓐ $\frac{3}{4} \times 9$

( )

Ⓑ $\frac{4}{9} \times \frac{3}{7}$

( )

Ⓒ $\frac{3}{8} \times \frac{4}{15}$

( )

Ⓓ $12 \times \frac{5}{9}$

( )

Ⓔ $\frac{3}{4} \times 1\frac{5}{7}$

( )

Ⓕ $2\frac{2}{3} \times 4\frac{1}{5}$

( )

2 Write appropriate inequality signs (>, <) in the ☐s below to show the relationship between $\frac{7}{8}$ and the size of products with $\frac{7}{8}$ as a factor. (10 points each)

Ⓐ $\frac{7}{8} \times 1.09$ ☐ $\frac{7}{8}$

Ⓑ $\frac{7}{8} \times \frac{6}{7}$ ☐ $\frac{7}{8}$

Ⓒ $\frac{7}{8} \times 1\frac{1}{6}$ ☐ $\frac{7}{8}$

Ⓓ $\frac{7}{8} \times \frac{7}{8}$ ☐ $\frac{7}{8}$

3 Answer the following questions. (15 points each)

Ⓐ The weight of 1 m of electric wire is 120 g. What is the weight of $1\frac{3}{5}$ m of electric wire in grams?

( )

Ⓑ The weight of a 1 m iron pipe is $3\frac{3}{4}$ kg. What is the weight of a $2\frac{1}{3}$ m iron pipe in kilograms?

( )

87

Multiplication of Fractions (Part 2)

1 Calculate the following. (10 points eatch)

Ⓐ $\frac{7}{8} \times \frac{1}{2} \times \frac{3}{4}$

Ⓑ $1\frac{2}{9} \times \frac{3}{7} \times 2\frac{1}{4}$

( )

( )

Ⓒ $\frac{5}{6} \times 2\frac{2}{5} \times 6\frac{2}{3}$

Ⓓ $\frac{5}{7} \times 18 \times \frac{9}{10}$

( )

( )

Ⓔ $27 \times \frac{10}{21} \times 1\frac{5}{9}$

Ⓕ $2\frac{2}{3} \times 0.125 \times 3\frac{1}{6}$

( )

( )

2 Find the volume of the following solids. (10 points each)

Ⓐ The volume of a cube with edges of $2\frac{2}{3}$ cm.

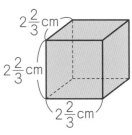

( )

Ⓑ The volume of a rectangular prism that has a $\frac{3}{4}$ m width, a 3 m length and a $1\frac{4}{9}$ m height.

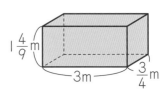

( )

3 You are going to paint a wall blue. To paint 1 m² of wall you need $\frac{3}{4}$ dL (deciliter) of paint. How many dL of paint do you need to paint a wall that is 1.5 m high and $2\frac{4}{5}$ m wide? (20 points)

( )

A deciliter ("dL") is a unit of liquid volume. 1 dL is $\frac{1}{10}$ of 1L (liter). 1 L is equal to 1000 mL (milliliter); therefore 1 dL is equal to 100 mL.

Let's Help Our Friends!

1 When you are having difficulty understanding mathematics, you are happy when your friends offer to help you. So, it will be even better if you help your friends when they are having difficulty, too! When you try to help a friend, you gain the added benefit of deepening your own understanding of the math topic your friend and you are discussing.

Look at the example below and help your friends think about problems Ⓐ through Ⓒ that are difficult for them to answer. [30 points for Ⓐ and Ⓑ, 40 points for Ⓒ]

[Example]

A problem your friend is having:

I used algorithm calculation to find the answer for 3.5 + 14.05, but my answer is incorrect.

$$\begin{array}{r} 3.5 \\ +\,1\,4.0\,5 \\ \hline 4.9\,0\,5 \end{array}$$

How to help:

It is important to think about place values and align each number's place values correctly. When you align decimal points, like place values are also aligned. So, now your calculations allow you to easily find the correct answer.

$$\begin{array}{r} 3.5 \\ +\,1\,4.0\,5 \\ \hline 1.7\,5\,5 \end{array}$$

Ⓐ **Another problem your friend is having:**

I added both denominators and both numerators, but my answer does not make sense, so it must be incorrect because $\frac{2}{5}$ is less than $\frac{1}{2}$.

$$\frac{1}{2}+\frac{1}{3}=\frac{2}{5}$$

How to help:

90

B

Another problem your friend is having:

12.34 ÷ 5.6 = 2.2 R 0.2

I used the algorithm shown to the right to find the quotient. I thought I did the calculation correctly, but it is incorrect.

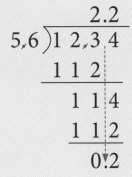

```
        2.2
5,6 )1 2,3 4
    1 1 2
    1 1 4
    1 1 2
      0 2
```

How to help:

C

Another problem your friend is having:

The calculation 2.5 × 0.27 × 4 + 2.7 × 9 was difficult.

2.5 × 0.27 × 4 = 0.675 × 4 = 2.7
2.7 × 9 = 24.3

So, 2.7 + 24.3 = 27.
My friend Yang found the answer very quickly. Is there a better way to calculate this problem?

How to help:

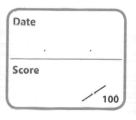

Date

Score

/100

1 Mr. Taylor, a 5th grade teacher, gave Louis some problems on volume of solid figures.

Mr. Taylor: Let's find the volume of this rectangular prism.
Louis: Sure!

Ⓐ How many cubic centimeters (cm³) is the volume of this rectangular prism? (20 points)

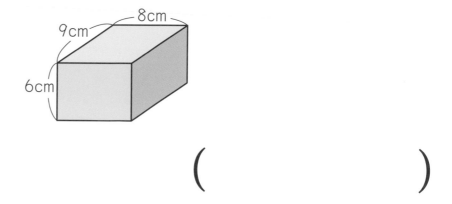

(   )

Mr. Taylor   : How about this solid? Do you know what it is called?

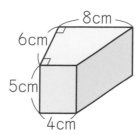

Louis   : It's a kind of prism and has a trapezoid base… So, is it a quadrangular prism?
Mr. Taylor : Yes. Then, can you find the volume?
Louis   : I don't know how.
Mr. Taylor : You will not learn how to find the volume of this type of solid figure in the 5th grade, but if you carefully think about how you might find the volume, you may find you can reason through be to find it. For example, if you combine two exactly the same solids, you may be able to find the volume. What do you think?
Louis   : I see! Thinking in this way I can see how to use the volume of a rectangular prism.

Ⓑ How many cubic centimeters (cm³) is the volume of the quadrangular prism? (20 points)

(   )

2 What are the names of the following solids? What are the volumes of these solids? (for the name, 10 points each; for the volume, 20 points each)

Ⓐ

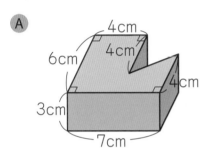

Name of the solid (   )

Volume (   )

Ⓑ

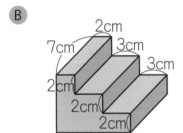

Name of the solid (   )

Volume (   )

Hint

Refer to problem **1** as you think about how to solve these problems. Think about how you can make a rectangular prism from the solid you are given.

1 Nadine, Takeshi, and Amy tried to solve a challenging problem about the volume of a solid.

This solid looks like a "cross." What is the volume of this solid?

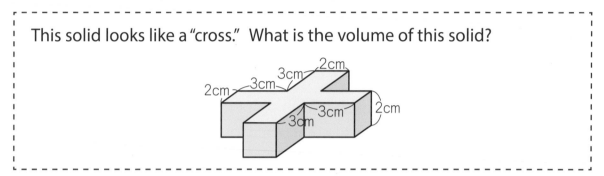

All of them found the solid's volume. Each person explained his/her own solution, as follows.

Nadine: I found the volume by splitting the solid into four rectangular prisms and a cube.

Takeshi: I thought about a large rectangular prism that includes this solid. Then I removed the parts that were not part of the original figure.

Amy: I looked at it as two long rectangular prisms that cross each other. I paid attention to the part where these prisms overlap.

A Which of the following math sentence represents each person's solution? (10 points each)

      a. $8 \times 8 \times 2 - (3 \times 3 \times 2) \times 4$

      b. $2 \times 8 \times 2 + (2 \times 3 \times 2) \times 2$

      c. $(2 \times 8 \times 2) \times 2 - 2 \times 2 \times 2$

      d. $(2 \times 3 \times 2) \times 4 + 2 \times 2 \times 2$

Nadine $\big($ $\big)$

Takeshi $\big($ $\big)$

Amy $\big($ $\big)$

(B) Find the volume of the solid. (20 points)

$$\Big($$ $\Big)$ cm³

2 There is a cube with 8 cm edges. Now, we will make a square hole that passes through from one side to the other side, as shown on the right. The dimension of the square opening is 2 cm by 2 cm and its location runs from the center of one of the faces through to the center of the opposite face.

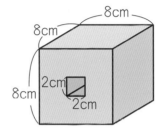

(A) Find the volume of the solid. (20 points)

$$\Big(\hspace{6cm} \Big)$$

(B) Next, we will make one more square hole with sides of 2 cm on the adjacent face of the cube which also passes through to the center of the opposite face. Find the volume of this solid. (30 points)

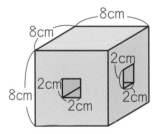

$$\Big(\hspace{6cm} \Big)$$

Hint

Think about the what the holes look like inside the cube. You have already seen this shape before.

Z-kai
Zoom-Up Workbook
Math
Answers and Solutions

Grade 5

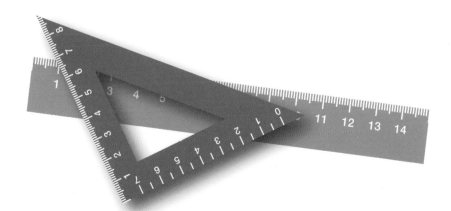

How to use Answers and Solutions Section

Point 1:

`Answers` Lists correct answers to all problems.

Point 2:

`How to Think and Solve` Discusses thinking and solution processes.

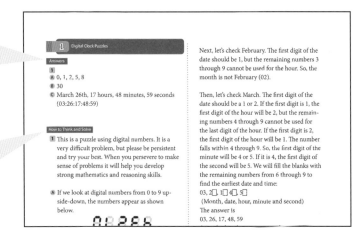

Problems in the Zoom-Up Workbook are not limited to the typical grade level content you learn in most math classes; however, many problems are solvable using mathematics knowledge and skills you have learned so far, if you know how to apply what you know. Most Zoom-Up problems are challenging, but the problems will help you develop problem solving skills, logical reasoning skills, explanation skills and perseverance.

When you solve these problems successfully, your confidence for learning mathematics will increase and you will become a great problem solver and a young mathematician!

❶ Please check your answers carefully and think about the solutions discussed in the "Answers and Solutions" section.

❷ Then score and add up the points according to the points guide given in each problem.

❸ If you made a mistake, read "How to Think and Solve" carefully and reflect on your solution process. Do not erase your mistakes; instead, keep a record of each error. Use a different color pen when you revise the solution and write down a clear explanation of how you made each mistake. What was your thinking and why was it incorrect? What things do you want to be sure to remember the next time? You will learn so much more if you think carefully and take your time to record what you have learned!

Dear parents, Dear teachers,

This "Answers and Solutions" section of the Zoom-Up Workbook explains answers and gives helpful points for thinking about and solving each problem. Dctailed solution processes are included for most of the challenging problems. Although the Zoom-Up Workbook is designed for students to study challenging problems on their own, it is helpful if parents and teachers read this book and support a student's learning by discussing the details. It may be helpful to provide clues that will help students understand solution processes. The book contains very challenging problems, so it is important for parents and teachers to encourage students' interest in solving problems and to enjoy the challenge.

Answers

1

Ⓐ 0, 1, 2, 5, 8

Ⓑ 30

Ⓒ March 26th, 17 hours, 48 minutes, 59 seconds
(03:26:17:48:59)

How to Think and Solve

1 This is a puzzle using digital numbers. It is a very difficult problem, but please be persistent and try your best. When you persevere to make sense of problems it will help you develop strong mathematics and reasoning skills.

Ⓐ If we look at digital numbers from 0 to 9 upside-down, the numbers appear as shown below.

Ⓑ Let the hundreds digit be ○, the ones digit be △, and the pair be (○, △). Then, we see there are six pairs that satisfy this condition:
(1, 1), (2, 2), (5, 5), (8, 8), (6, 9) and (9, 6).
If we rotate 6 and 9, they can be seen as 9 and 6. So, we should check (6, 9) and (9, 6).
For the tens digit, we can use the numbers found in Ⓐ : 0, 1, 2, 5 and 8.
Finally, each pair has five ways to place the tens' digit number;
so, 5 × 6 = 30.

Ⓒ Since we want to find the earliest date and time, start checking from January (01). In this case, only 23 can be used for the hour (using a 24-hour clock). The remaining numbers 4 through 9 cannot be used for the date. So, the month is not January (01).

Next, let's check February. The first digit of the date should be 1, but the remaining numbers 3 through 9 cannot be used for the hour. So, the month is not February (02).

Then, let's check March. The first digit of the date should be a 1 or 2. If the first digit is 1, the first digit of the hour will be 2, but the remaining numbers 4 through 9 cannot be used for the last digit of the hour. If the first digit is 2, the first digit of the hour will be 1. The number falls within 4 through 9. So, the first digit of the minute will be 4 or 5. If it is 4, the first digit of the second will be 5. We will fill the blanks with the remaining numbers from 6 through 9 to find the earliest date and time:
03, 2☐, 1☐ 4☐, 5☐
(Month, date, hour, minute and second)
The answer is
03, 26, 17, 48, 59
(Month, date, hour, minute and second)
March 26th, 17 hours, 48 minutes, 59 seconds

Answers

1

Ⓐ **Math Sentence:** $1 + 7 = 8$, $4 \times 8 \div 2 = 16$
Answer: 16

Ⓑ The number of seashells in the 50th row: 99
Total number of seashells: 2,500

2 125,250

How to Think and Solve

1 This is a math problem that asks for a better way to find the sum of an arithmetic progression (e.g., 1, 3, 5, 7, …).

Ⓐ When objects are arranged and aligned in a staircase shape, you can put two identical staircase shapes together and form a rectangle. With a rectangular shapes, it is easy to use multiplication to find the number of objects comprising the rectangle. The number of objects that are in the original single staircase shape is one half of the number of objects in the composite rectangle, so dividing the number by 2 gives us the number of objects that comprise the staircase.

If you have a number of seashells aligned and arranged in a 4-step staircase and you put together two identical staircases, the height will be 4 seashells and the length will be $1 + 7 = 8$ seashells. So, the total number of seashells will be $4 \times 8 \div 2 = 16$ seashells.

Ⓑ

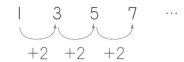

The best way to solve this problem is to figure out how many times you need to add two (2) to one seashell in the first top row, and so on, in order to find the number of seashells in the 50th row.

In the 2nd row, there are 3 seashells. The sum is 1 seashell in the 1st row and $(2 - 1)$ times 2 seashells.

In the 3rd row, there are 5 seashells. This means the sum will be 1 seashell in the 1st row and $(3 - 1)$ times 2 seashells.

In the 4th row, there are 7 seashells. This means the sum will be 1 seashell in the 1st row and $(4 - 1)$ times 2 seashells.

Therefore, to find the number of shells in the 50th row, the number will be the sum of 1 seashell in the 1st row and $(50 - 1)$ times 2 seashells. So, there are $1 + 2 \times (50 - 1) = 99$ seashells in the 50th row.

In order to find the total number of seashells in the 50-step staircase, we can use the strategy we used in problem Ⓐ.

If we put together two identical 50-step staircases, a rectangle is formed with a height of 50 seashells and a width of $1 + 99 = 100$ seashells. Therefore, the total number of seashells in one 50-step staircase is $50 \times 100 \div 2 = 2,500$ seashells.

2 Find the whole numbers from 1 to 1,000 whose divisor is 4 and remainder is 3, then put these whole numbers in sequential order from the least to the greatest. The number sequence will look like the sequence shown below.

The sequence of numbers increases constantly by adding 4. The pattern of this increase in number is similar to the pattern in problem **1** **A**. Therefore, to find the number of rows calculate:
$999 = 3 + 4 \times (250 - 1)$
There are 250 numbers of rows.

To find the number of numbers in a bottom row calculate:
$3 + 999 = 1,002$ (numbers).
The 1st top row has 3 numbers and the 250th row has 999 numbers.
Next we can make a rectangle using two identical staircases.
So, the total number of whole numbers can be found by calculating
$250 \times 1,002 \div 2 = 125,250$ (numbers)

Answers

1
Ⓐ ① $150,000,000 \div 300 = 500,000$ (150 million ÷ 300 = 0.5 million or 500 thousand)
② 500,000 (500 thousand)
Ⓑ ③ 3,600,000
(3 million, 600 thousand; 3.6 million)
Ⓒ ④ $60 \times 60 \times 24 \times 365 = 31,536,000$
$300,000 \times 31,536,000 = 9,460,800,000,000$ or 9 trillion, 460 billion, 800 million
⑤ About 9 trillion, 500 billion (9.5 trillion)
Ⓓ **Math Sentence:**
9 trillion, 500 billion ÷ 1 trillion, 500 billion = 63,333.3 …
Answer:
approximately 63,000 astronomical units.

How to Think and Solve

1 The problem requires an understanding of large numbers (Grade 5), unit rate, and speed (Grade 6). You may not have learned about these 6th grade topics, but why not challenge yourself? The problem covers interesting but unimaginable sizes of measurement units such as "light years" and "astronomical units." I hope you become interested and motivated to learn about large numbers and large measurement units, while developing calculation skills with large numbers and learning the importance of unit conversion.

B The Shinkansen (bullet train) travels 300 km in 1 hour (60 minutes). So, the distance the Shinkansen can travel in 1 minute is: $300 \div 60 = 5$ (km)

Light travels 300,000 km in 1 second. So, the distance light travels in 1 minute (60 seconds) is:

$300,000 \times 60 = 18,000,000$ (km)

$18,000,000 \div 5 = 3,600,000$

So, the speed of light is 3,600,000 times faster than the speed of the Shinkansen.

C 60 seconds = 1 minute

60 minutes = 1 hour

24 hours = 1 day

Therefore, 1 year measured in seconds is $60 \times 60 \times 24 \times 365 = 31,536,000$ (seconds).

If light travels 300,000 km in 1 second, the distance light travels in a year is: $300,000 \times 31,536,000 = 9,460,800,000,000$ (km) (9 trillion, 536 billion, 800 million km)

D When units are converted, we can see that 1 astronomical unit equals 150,000,000 km and 1 light year equals 9,500,000,000,000 km.

Answers

1

A 1,000,000,000 B (1 billion bytes)

B 12 B (12 bytes)

C **Math Sentence:** $700 \div 3 = 233$ R1

Answer: 233 photos

D D and E

How to Think and Solve

1

A 1 GB = 1,000 MB

1 MB = 1,000 kB

1 kB = 1,000 B

So, 1 GB is:

$1,000 \times 1,000 \times 1,000 = 1,000,000,000$ (B)

(1 billion bytes)

B The sentence "12本のＨＢ鉛筆" has two alphabet characters and two numbers. An alphabet character or a number each use 1 byte. The sentence also includes four Japanese characters (hiragana and kanji). Each Japanese character uses 2 bytes.

So, the total number of bytes used for the sentence above is: $1 \times (2 + 2) + 2 \times 4 = 12$ (B)

C $700 \div 3 = 233$ R1. This tells us that when you save 233 pictures on a 700 MB CD, 1 MB of space will be left over. With only this 1 MB of space you can't save another 3 MB photo, so the answer is 233 photos.

It is okay for the sentence to be written as $700 \div 3 = 233.3 \dots$

D 1 hour 10 minutes = 70 minutes

So, the size of the movie Rachel's father wants to record is: $112 \times 70 = 7,840$ (MB)

1,000 MB = 1 GB

7,840 MB = 7.84 GB

103

The SD cards that can record 7.84 GB of movie data are D (8 GB) and E (16 GB) SD cards.

The metric prefix such as "kilo-," "mega-," and "giga-" denote important units. For this problem, you learned how you can show the data size using these units.

1,000 times 1 B is 1 kB, 1,000,000 times 1 B is 1 MB, and 1,000,000,000 times 1B is 1 GB.

Knowing metric prefixes and unit relationships is useful for your future study of measurement, so be sure you remember the relationships among units and the abbreviations for units.

Answers

1

Ⓐ ① 3   ② 2

Ⓑ [Example]

Start measuring the time interval right after the 5-minute hourglass is flipped 3 times (10 minutes from the starting first flip) and end measuring the time interval when the 8-minute hourglass is flipped 3 times (16 minutes from the start). Using this method, Sarah can measure 6 minutes.

Ⓒ 20 minutes

How to Think and Solve

1

Ⓐ ① You are measuring the time interval from the end of a 5-minute hourglass to the end of an 8-minute hourglass.
So, ① is a time interval of 8 – 5 = 3 (minutes).

② Here you are measuring the time interval from the end of an 8-minute hourglass to the end of the second time interval of the 5-minute hourglass (that is, 5 min × 2, or 10 minutes have elapsed).
So, ② is a time interval of 10 – 8 = 2 (minutes).

Ⓑ Carefully study the number line in the diagram labeled "Two hourglasses combined." Look for the place that aligns with the 6-minute interval on the number line. When you flip a 5-minute hourglass three times (including the first flip to start measuring time), you can measure 10 minutes. When you flip the 8-minute hourglass three times (including the first flip to start measuring time), you can measure 16 minutes. So, you can measure 6 minutes by subtracting them: 16 – 10 = 6 (minutes).

This is one way to measure 6 minutes. There are also more ways to measure 6 minutes. For example, if you start measuring time after flipping the 8-minute hourglass four times (which measures 24 minutes), you will be able to measure a time interval of 6 minutes between that 24-minute point and the point when the 5-minute hourglass is empty for the sixth time (when 30 min has passed): therefore, 30 − 24 = 6 (minutes).

If your response demonstrates an understanding of the starting and the ending points of measurement, the response is correct.

C If we note all intervals on a multiple number line as represented in question B , we can visually represent the following times in minutes: 0, 5, 8, 10, 15, 16, 20, 24, 25, 30, 32, 35, ….

Using these results, we can calculate 8 different time intervals from 1 minute through 8 minutes.

1 minute:
16 − 15 = 1
16 elapsed min to measure a 1-min difference

2 minutes:
10 − 8 = 2
10 elapsed min to measure this a 2-min difference

3 minutes:
8 − 5 = 3
8 elapsed min to measure a 3-min difference

4 minutes:
20 − 16 = 4
20 elapsed min to measure a 4-min difference

5 minutes:
5 − 0 = 5
5 elapsed min, of course!

6 minutes:
16 − 10 = 6
16 elapsed min to measure a 6-min difference

7 minutes:
15 − 8 = 7
15 elapsed min to measure a 7-min difference

8 minutes:
8 − 0 = 8
8 elapsed min, of course!

The last time interval that we can measure is 4 minutes and it will take 20 elapsed minutes.

Furthermore, by knowing we can measure 1 minute by 16 − 15 = 1, we can say that we can measure all minute-intervals. For example, if we want to measure 11 minutes, we can multiply both 16 minutes and 15 minutes by 11 since the difference between them is 1 minute.
$16 \times 11 - 15 \times 11 = 11$ (11 minutes) This means that we can measure 11 minutes at $16 \times 11 = 176$ minutes of elapsed time. However, since we can measure 11 minutes by finding the difference between 16 minutes and 5 minutes, 16 − 5 = 11, we don't need to wait 176 minutes to measure 11 minutes.

Answers

1

*Process of algorithm calculations are omitted.

(A) 2   (B) 2   R11   (C) 3   R10

(D) 7   R5   (E) 6   R7   (F) 6   R3

(G) 4   R3   (H) 5   R8

2

(A)
$$\begin{array}{r} 6 \\ 16{\overline{)96}} \\ 96 \\ \hline 0 \end{array}$$

(B)
$$\begin{array}{r} 4 \\ 23{\overline{)97}} \\ 92 \\ \hline 5 \end{array}$$

3

(A) 5, 6, 7, 8, 9   (B) 8, 9

How to Think and Solve

1 If you consider a temporary quotient, it will be easier to find an answer.

(B) Think about the dividend as 80 and the divisor as 30, then carry out the calculation 80 ÷ 30 = 2 R20. From this, think about using 2 as a temporary quotient.

$$\begin{array}{r} 2 \\ 34{\overline{)79}} \\ 68 \\ \hline 11 \end{array}$$

(D) Think about the dividend as 80 and the divisor as 10, then 80 ÷ 10 = 8. From this, use 8 as a temporary quotient, 11 × 8 = 88. The number 88 is too large to be subtracted from 82, so we need to make the quotient one smaller (from 8 to 7).

$$\begin{array}{r} 8 \\ 11{\overline{)82}} \\ 88 \end{array} \longrightarrow \begin{array}{r} 7 \\ 11{\overline{)82}} \\ 77 \\ \hline 5 \end{array}$$

Cannot subtract   Make the quotient 1 smaller

(F) Think about the dividend as 90 and the divisor as 20, then calculate 90 ÷ 20 = 4 R10. From this, consider using 4 as a temporary quotient: 15 × 4 = 60, 93 – 60 = 33. The remainder 33 is

larger than the quotient, so make the temporary quotient larger by one until reaching the appropriate quotient value.

$$\begin{array}{r} 4 \\ 15{\overline{)93}} \\ 60 \\ \hline 33 \end{array} \longrightarrow \begin{array}{r} 6 \\ 15{\overline{)93}} \\ 90 \\ \hline 3 \end{array}$$

The remainder is larger than the divisor   Make the temporary quotient one larger until appropriate

2

(A) [A] and [B] can be found using subtraction within the algorithm. [A] will be 6 and [B] will be 9, so the divisor can be justified by 96 ÷ 6 = 16.

$$\begin{array}{r} 6 \\ \square\square{\overline{)9[A]}} \\ [B]6 \\ \hline 0 \end{array}$$

(B) The ones place of [C] × 4 is 2, so [C] should be 3 or 8. If [C] is 8, 28 × 4 = 112. The dividend should be a 2- digit not a 3-digit number, so 8 does not fit in [C]. Therefore, [C] is 3 and the dividend is 23 × 4 + 5 = 97.

$$\begin{array}{r} 4 \\ 2[C]{\overline{)\square\square}} \\ \square 2 \\ \hline 5 \end{array}$$

3

(A) When □6 part of the 3-digit number is greater than 53, the quotient will have to be a 2-digit number, because there will be a number in the tens place of the quotient. Because the quotient will be more than or equal to 10, the dividend is said to be more than or equal to 530 (53 × 10 = 530).

(B) When the □4 of the 3-digit number is greater than 76, the quotient will have to be a 2-digit number, because there will be a number in the tens place of the quotient. Because the quotient will be more than or equal to 10, the dividend is said to be more than or equal to 760 (76 × 10 = 760).

Answers

1

*Process of algorithm calculations are omitted.

A 7   B 9   C 8   R44

D 22   E 27   R7   F 37   R21

G 5   R7   H 186   R23

2

A
```
       98
59)5792
   531
    482
    472
     10
```

B
```
       56
37)2077
   185
    227
    222
      5
```

3 Quotient 62, Remainder 7

How to Think and Solve

1 The quotients of Problem D, E, and F start from the tens place.

D
```
       22
45)990
   90
    90
    90
     0
```

E
```
       27
35)952
   70
   252
   245
     7
```

F
```
       37
23)872
   69
   182
   161
    21
```

G Think about the dividend as 600 and the divisor as 100, then carry out the calculation 600 ÷ 100 = 6. From this, think about using 6 as a temporary quotient, 123 × 6 = 738. 738 cannot be subtracted from 622 so we need to make the quotient one smaller.

```
        6                          5
123)622         →        123)622
    738                          615
                                   7
```

Cannot subtract   Make the quotient 1 smaller

H 59 is larger than 32 so the calculation of the quotient starts from the hundreds place. The process of calculating is the same as when the dividend was a 2-digit or 3-digit number.

```
        186
32)5975
   32
   277
   256
    215
    192
     23
```

2

A 5 $\boxed{A}$$\boxed{B}$ – 531 = 48 So, $\boxed{A}$ should be 7 and $\boxed{B}$ should be 9. Other numbers that go into □s can be found by calculating 5792 ÷ 59.

```
        □□
59)5□□2
   531□
    482
     47
     10
```

B From the algorithm calcluation to the right, 3□ × $\boxed{C}$ = 185. One-digit numbers that could divide 185 completely are either 1 or 5, but 5 is the only number that satisfies the sentence above. So, $\boxed{C}$ is 5 and the divisor is 185 ÷ 5 = 37. The dividend can be found by how many numbers are subtracted, □□□ – 222 = 5, so the bottom □□□s can be found by 222 + 5 = 227. With □□□ – 185 = 22, the first three digits of the dividend □□□ can be found by calculating 185 + 22 = 207. The last digit of the dividend is 7. The quotient can be found by calculating 222 ÷ 37 = 6.

Another method to find the dividend is first to find the ones place of the quotient, 222 ÷ 37 = 6. Now we know that □□□□ ÷ 37 = 56 R5, so 56 × 37 + 5 = 2077. This method is used for checking the calculation of division with a remainder.

```
         C□
3□)□□□□
   185
   □□□
   222
     5
```

3 If you make the unknown number □, □ ÷ 6 = 83 R5. When we check this calculation we can rewrite this sentence as 6 × 83 + 5 = □. So □ is found to be 503. When we calculate this problem correctly, the calculation becomes 503 ÷ 8 = 62 R7.

Answers

1

Ⓐ [Example]

Name the two incense sticks A and B. Stick A will be lit from both ends simultaneously and stick B will be lit from one end only. We will start measuring time by lighting both sticks at the same time. When stick A burns out (10" elapsed), we will light the other end of stick B. When stick B burns out (5" elapsed), we have measured the elapsed time 15 minutes from the beginning.

Ⓑ 45 minutes and 50 minutes

2

Ⓐ [Example]

Light the 2-minute incense stick from the both ends simultaneously and measure the elapsed time from the beginning.

Ⓑ [Example]

Light the 6-minute incense stick from only one end. When the 6-minute stick burns out, light the 3-minute stick from only one end. When the 3-minute stick burns out, light the 2-minute stick from both ends. When the 2-minute stick burns out, we have measured 10 minutes of elapsed time from the beginning (from the time we lit the first stick) .

How to Think and Solve

1

Ⓐ Name the two incense sticks A and B. First light both ends of stick A and only one end of stick B simultaneously.

A ▬▬▬▬▬▬▬▬▬▬
B ▬▬▬▬▬▬▬▬▬▬

When stick A burns out, light the other end of stick B. The elapsed time is 10 minutes at this point from the beginning.

A ▬▬▬▬▬▬▬▬▬▬
B ▬▬▬▬▬▬▬▬▬▬

When stick B burns out, 5 min of elapsed time is added to the previous elapsed time of 10 minutes. Since a half-length of stick B is burning from the both ends, it takes only 5 minutes for the stick to burn out.

The total elapsed time from beginning to end is 10 + 5 = 15 (minutes).

To get full points for this problem, you need to describe clearly when, which, and what part(s) of the sticks are lit.

Ⓑ We can measure various elapsed time periods using incense sticks to solve problem Ⓐ:

   5 minutes: using two incense sticks
   10 minutes: using one incense stick
   15 minutes: using two incense sticks
   20 minutes: using one incense stick

So, we can measure other elapsed time periods, as shown below:

   25 minutes: using three incense sticks
   (20 + 5 minutes or 10 + 15 minutes)
   30 minutes: using two incense sticks
   (20 + 10 minutes)
   35 minutes: using three incense sticks
   (20 + 15 minutes)
   40 minutes: using two incense sticks
   (20 × 2 minutes)
   50 minutes: using three incense sticks
   (20 × 2 + 10 minutes)
   60 minutes: using three incense sticks
   (20 × 3 minutes)

To measure 40 minutes of elapsed time, we need two incense sticks. You also need two incense sticks to measure 5- and 15-minute

108

elapsed time periods; therefore, we cannot measure 45 and 55 minutes by using fewer than three incense sticks.

2 This question requires an understanding of which and when the two incense sticks should be lit:

Ⓐ Think and solve the problem in a similar way to what we did in problem **1**.

Ⓑ If we burn each stick successively from one side, the total elapsed time will be 2 + 3 + 6 = 11 (minutes). It is one minute more than 10 minutes. We found in the previous problem that we can measure one minute by using a 2-minutes incense stick and light it from both ends Ⓐ.

Answers

1

Ⓐ [Example]
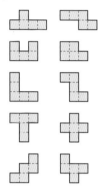

Ⓑ [Example] There are 10 ways to compose a 5-square figure, as shown below.

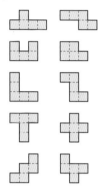

How to Think and Solve

1

Ⓐ If you rotate the rectangle you will see the same two 5-square shapes. If you thought about splitting the rectangle as shown below, that is the correct third way to split the rectangle.

Ⓑ You may randomly think of 5-square figures that are different, but if you think logically in an organized manner, it will become easier to investigate. So, now let's investigate by thinking about the number of squares aligned horizontally to start. Recognize that only Figure A that Natalia initially found has five squares aligned horizontally.

Think about making a 5-square figure starting with 4 squares in a line. Let's think about where we can add the fifth square. If you look at the diagram on the next page, you can see that you can't make a different shape by adding another square where there are Xs. When a square is added in box A, it will be the same shape as figure B that Natalia initially found.

If a square is added in box B, then you can create a different shape which looks like the figure below.

If you put the fifth square in any of the C boxes and rotate or flip the shape, you will see the same shape as either figure B (that Natalia initially found) or the figure shown above (when a square was added in box B).

Next, let's use the diagram below to check shapes that start with 3 squares in a row. If you put a fourth square in box D in the diagram shown below, the only possible places you can put the last square are in the E boxes. From this, we can find 7 figures.

Similarly, if we add a square in box F in the diagram below, the last square can be placed in box G. Adding box F will give us only one more shape, as shown below:

Now let's check to see what happens when you start with only two squares. We can make only one more different 5-square shape shown below.

You may find a figure that looks different from the figures above. Be sure to rotate or flip your figures to see if your figure matches with the figure. If your shape matches, then it is correct.

Answers

1

Ⓐ ① ✓Yes   ② ✗No   ③ ✗No   ④ ✓Yes

Ⓑ [Example]

Let the area of a square be 1 cm². Since the area of each of the figures A to L is 5 cm², the sum of the area of any combination of these figures must be a multiple of 5. The area of the rectangle that is made up of squares in 4 rows and 6 columns is 24 cm², which is not a multiple of 5. Therefore, it is not possible to fill this 4 × 6 rectangle using any combination of figures A to L.

Ⓒ

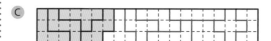

How to Think and Solve

1

Ⓐ ① The rectangle can be filled with the shapes B, D, and G as shown below.

② It's impossible to fill this rectangle using shapes F, I and L. If figure L is positioned so that one side aligns to the rectangle's right or left side, it will leave some spaces unfilled. This means the only possible place to put figure L is in the center. However, when figure L is placed in the center and rotated or flipped, the two remaining unfilled areas cannot be filled by figures F and I.

③ All three figures will leave spaces unfilled when they are positioned to align with the right or the left sides of the rectangle. So, the figures cannot fill the rectangle with the shapes H, J and K.

④ The rectangle can be filled with the shapes C, E, and F as shown below.

Ⓑ Problem Ⓑ is a difficult problem that requires an explanation of why we can't fill the 6 by 4 rectangle. Even if you try to place pieces and explain your thinking, the task will be a difficult one, because it looks like there are many different ways to fill the rectangle. So, let's explore an explanation using a characteristic of the shapes as a group (rather than investigating each shape one at a time).

Let's focus on the fact that all figures A to L do not have the same shape, but do have the same area with 5 squares. Let the area of a square be 1 cm². If the rectangle is filled with some combination of shapes A to L, the area of the sum of these shapes would have to be a multiple of 5 cm². However, the area of the rectangle is 6 × 4 = 24 (cm²), which is not a multiple of 5. So, it's clear that the rectangle cannot be filled by using any combination of these figures.

Ⓒ This is a problem that requires tenacious thinking, using logical trial and error to find the solution. You will find clues by thinking about and using the characteristics of the shapes. For example,

- Since the rectangle has 3 rows, the figures A, B and D must be placed horizontally. (Figure C is already placed inside the rectangle.)
- No matter how figure J is rotated, it will have the same shape. (So, we know that shape J will have a place somewhere in the rectangle.)
- As written above in problem Ⓐ: If figure J or figure L is aligned with the right side of the rectangle, there will be some spaces left unfilled. So, these figures must not be aligned with the right side.

Remember, it's important to use these clues to think about the solution.

Answers

1

Ⓐ ① 1,000   ② 1,001   ③ 143

Ⓑ [Example]

If we represent the 6-digit number with ●▲● ▲●▲, a math sentence can be established.

●▲●▲●▲ = ●▲ × 10,101

10101 ÷ 7 = 1,443

10101 can be divided by 7.

So, ●▲●▲●▲ is a multiple of 7.

How to Think and Solve

1

Ⓐ This is a challenge problem that requires you to explain why Benjamin's description about multiples is correct.

If we split 123,123 by its repeating pattern: 123/123, then we can use the distributive property of multiplication,

$\bigcirc \times \triangle + \bigcirc \times \square = \bigcirc \times (\triangle + \square)$.

$\quad$ 123,123

$= 123,000 + 123$

$= 123 \times 1,000 + 123 \times 1$

$= 123 \times (1,000 + 1)$

$= 123 \times 1,001$

Given 1,001 ÷ 7 = 143, it is true that 1,001 has 7 as a factor. 123,123 also has 7 as a factor, so it is a multiple of 7.

For ●▲■●▲■,

$\quad$ ●▲■●▲■,

$=$ ●▲■ 000 + ●▲■

$=$ ●▲■ × 1,000 + ●▲■ × 1

$=$ ●▲■ × (1,000 + 1)

$=$ ●▲■ × 1,001

Therefore, ●▲■●▲■ is also a multiple of 7, just as 123,123 is a multiple of 7.

111

B Let's think about 121212. If we split 121,212 by its repeating pattern: 12/12/12.

121,212
= 120,000 + 1,200 + 12
= 12 × 10,000 + 12 × 100 + 12 × 1
= 12 × (10,000 + 100 + 1)
= 12 × 10,101

Given 10,101 ÷ 7 = 1,443, it is true that 10,101 is divisible by 7, and 121,212 is a multiple of 7.

Therefore, we can explain this fact by replacing 121,212 with ●▲●▲●▲.
If the two following explanations are included in your response, you get 20 points for each.

- ●▲●▲●▲ = ●▲ × 10,101
- 10,101 can be divided by 7

The sentence ●▲●▲●▲ = ●▲ × 10,101 is thought of as follows:

●▲●▲●▲
= ●▲ 0000 + ●▲ 00 + ●▲
= ●▲ × 10,000 + ●▲ × 100 +●▲ × 1
= ●▲ × (10,000 + 100 + 1)
= ●▲ × 10,101

Answers

1

A 46,822,864, 82,466,428

B 2

C If the last six digits are 000,000 or are a multiple of 64 or "000,000," then the number is a multiple of 64.

2

A [Example]
The difference between the sum of all the numbers in odd number locations starting from the left and the sum of the numbers in even number locations starting from the left of 18181818181818181 is 8 × 8 − 1 × 9 = 55.
55 is a multiple of 11, so 18181818181818181 is also a multiple of 11.

B 10,263

How to Think and Solve

1

A We can determine whether a number is a multiple of 4 by examining if the last two digits are a multiple of 4 or the number ends with two zeroes, 00.

24,688,642
46,822,864
68,244,286
82,466,428

B We can determine whether a number is a multiple of 8 by examining if the last three digits of a number are a multiple of 8 or are 000.

12,345,67☐

→ Find a multiple of 8 in the numbers 670 through 679.
Since the multiples of 8 are the multiples of 4, all you have to do is examine the numbers 672 and 676. These are the only two numbers be-

tween 670 and 679 with multiples of 4 as the last two digits.

C Think about Benjamin's research and the "divisibility rules" table he found at the library. The four rules listed in the table help you figure out if a given number is a multiple of 2, 4, 8, or 16. So, now we must figure out what rule will tell us whether a number is a multiple of 64. First look at the rules in the table. Each number is a product of multiplying 2 several times. For example, 2 is 2, 4 is 2×2, 8 is $2 \times 2 \times 2$, and 16 is $2 \times 2 \times 2 \times 2$. In this sequence, each previous product is multiplied to 2 (so the number of 2s you are multiplying increases by one each time).

So, we need to think about where 64 is in the sequence described above. The rules also hold other information. Look at the number of last digits and the number of zeros. These numbers are also increasing. If the numbers above are products of 2 multiplied □ times, we have only to examine the last □ digits.

64 is multiplied by 2 six times.

2

A If the two following points are included in your response, you get 15 points for each.

- The difference between the sum of all the numbers in odd number locations from the left and the sum of the numbers in even number locations from the left is 55
- The difference, 55, is a multiple of 11.

B Let the smallest 5-digit number be 102●▲. (● and ▲ are different numbers and they the numbers will be 3 through 9.)

The sum of all the numbers in odd number locations from the left is:
$1 + 2 + ▲ = 3 + ▲$

The sum of all the numbers in even number locations from the left is:
$0 + ● = ●$

Since we want to find the smallest number possible, we will examine first the condition where the ● is 3 (the lowest of the numbers 3-9).
If ● is 3, the difference between the two sums will be ▲, but ▲ is neither a multiple of 11 nor 0 (that is, $3 + ▲ - 3 = ▲$).
If ● is 4, the difference between the two sums will be ▲ – 1, but ▲ – 1 is neither a multiple of 11 nor 0.
If ● is 5, the difference between the two sums will be ▲ – 2, but ▲ – 2 is neither a multiple of 11 nor 0.
If ● is 6, the difference between the two sums will be ▲ – 3. When ▲ is 3, ▲ – 3 becomes 0, which is a multiple of 11.
So, the smallest 5-digit number is 10,263.

Answers

1

Ⓐ **Math Sentence:** $40 \times 3 = 120$

$120 \div 16 = 7.5$

Answer: 7.5 g

Ⓑ **Math Sentence:** $10 + 3 + 7 = 20$

$10.5 \times 20 = 210$

Answer: 210 cents ($2.1)

Ⓒ **Math Sentence:** $93 \times 7 = 651$

$1,000 - 651 = 349$

Answer: 349 cents ($3.49)

Ⓓ ① 3.2　　② 96　　③ 78

How to Think and Solve

1

Ⓐ The total amount of chocolate is $40 \times 3 = 120$ (g)

Average = Total ÷ Number of units

So, the average weight of a chocolate bar is
$120 \div 16 = 7.5$ (g)

Ⓑ The total number of aluminum molds is
$10 + 3 + 7 = 20$ (aluminum molds)

Total = Average × Number of units

So, the total price of the aluminum molds is
$10.5 \times 20 = 210$ (cents)

She paid 2 dollars and 10 cents.

Ⓒ Total = Average × Number of units

So, when he buys 7 different kinds of chocolate,
$93 \times 7 = 651$ (cents)

It is 6 dollars and 51 cents.

If she paid with a 10 dollar bill, she will get $10
– $6.51 = $3.49 in change

Ⓓ ① Since 8 chocolates weigh for 25.6g, the average weight of a piece of chocolate is
$25.6 \div 8 = 3.2$ (g)

② Think about each piece of chocolate as 3.2g which we found as the average weight of a piece of chocolate in ①. The total weight of 30 chocolates can be found by
$3.2 \times 30 = 96$ (g)

③ Using the same method as above, let the weight of each chocolate be 3.2g.
Number of units = Total ÷ Average
$250 \div 3.2 = 78.1\ldots$
Rounding decimals at tenths to make a whole number, you will get 78 as the number of chocolates.
You can also write a sentence using □ as the number of chocolates.
The weight of □ number of chocolates is 250g. The average weight of each chocolate can be thought as 3.2g.

$250 \div \square = 3.2$

$250 = 3.2 \times \square$

$\square = 250 \div 3.2$

From this math sentence, we found the answer as 78 chocolates just as before.

Answers

A Math Sentence:

$210 \times 3 = 630$

$295 \times 2 = 590$

$630 + 590 = 1,220$

$1,220 \div 5 = 244$

Answer: 244 g

B ① 135   ② 20   ③ 2

④ greater (more)

How to Think and Solve

A First, we are going to find the total weight of 5 gifts of wrapped chocolates.

    Total = Average × Number of units

First, we find the total weight of 3 chocolate gifts that Olivia, Emma, and Maia prepared:

$210 \times 3 = 630(g)$

Then, find the total weight of 2 chocolate gifts that Theo and Liam prepared:

$295 \times 2 = 590(g)$

So, the total weight of 5 chocolate gifts is

$630 + 590 = 1,220(g)$

    Average = Total ÷ Number of units

So, $1,220 \div 5 = 244 \ (g)$

Although the average of 3 chocolate gifts is 210 g and that of 2 chocolate gifts is 295 g, the average of 5 gifts will not be $(210 + 295) \div 2 = 252.5$ (g).

That is, since 210 represents 3 chocolate gifts and 295 represents 2 chocolate gifts, we cannot treat 210 and 295 as if both averages represent the same number of units. Therefore, we need to find the total weight of 5 sets, before calculating to find the average.

B ① **Total = Average × Number of units**

So, the number of pieces of chocolates the five friends prepared would be:

$27 \times 5 = 135$ (chocolates)

② The number of pieces of chocolate prepared by the four children without including the number of pieces Liam prepared would be as follows:

$18 + 7 + 78 + 12 = 115$ (chocolates)

So, the number of pieces of chocolate Liam prepared is:

$135 - 115 = 20$ (chocolates)

③ If we put the number of pieces of chocolate they prepared in order from greatest to least, it is

78, 20, 18, 12, 7

So, Liam has the second greatest number of pieces of chocolate among the group.

④ His number of chocolates is the second highest among five friends, so his number falls within the higher end of the five numbers.

It is also important to note that if there is an extreme value (that is much larger than all other values) in a set of data, the average will be greater. This larger average results in larger differences between the average and the individual data values.

In this word problem, the value 78 is extremely greater than the other values. Therefore, the average of 27 is greater than 20, the second greatest value, and all other values in the group.

*Note: These extreme data values are called "outliers," because their values are very different from the other values in a set of data.

Answers

1 the 4th   **2** Wednesday the 6th

3 Suit: Diamond, Number: 12

How to Think and Solve

1 Make a table as shown below and put an "×" to identify impossible locations in birth order.

Since Summer was born after the dog that was born after Spring, Spring cannot be in either the 3rd or the 4th position in the birth order.

So, Summer cannot have been born 1st or 2nd.

Autumn cannot have been born 1st or 4th, because there is one dog that was born after and before her.

Winter cannot have not been born 1st, because he was born after Spring.

Order / Dog Name	Spring	Summer	Autumn	Winter
1st		×	×	×
2nd		×		
3rd	×			
4th	×		×	

The table shows that only Spring can be the 1st born.

When Spring is the 1st born, Summer will be the 3rd born.

Since Autumn cannot be 4th in the birth order, Autumn should be placed 2nd in the birth order. Finally, Winter was the 4th born.

2 From Benjamin's two statements, the 2nd and 4th days that Benjamin is not available Emilio is also not available. So, think about how to determine the days of the week that the 2nd and the 4th will fall on. Since the 3rd is between the 2nd and 4th and is available for both Benjamin and Emilio, we need to find the days of the week that have one day between them. Given that Emilio is not free on Monday, Tuesday, Friday, or Saturday, Sunday is the only day that falls between two days (Saturday and Monday). So, we can identify that the 2nd is a Saturday and the 4th is a Monday. Using this information, we can make a table to organize what we have found. To identify days when someone is not available, we put an "×" in those cells. For example, Ryan is available on even days only, so we put "×"s on his odd days.

Day of week / Name of people	Fri., 1st	Sat., 2nd	Sun., 3rd	Mon., 4th	Tue., 5th	Wed., 6th	Thu., 7th
Benjamin		×		×			
Emilio	×	×		×	×		
Ryan	×		×		×		×

From this table we can identify the only day they can play together, which is on Wednesday the 6th.

3 Below is the table from the problem.

Suit	Hearts	Clubs	Spades	Diamond
Numbers	1, 3, 12	11, 13	1, 8, 11	8, 12

Among the ten playing cards Emilio received, cards 3 and 13 appeared only once. If the suit is hearts or clubs, Benjamin thinks that Ryan will be able to figure it out. So, Benjamin said, "You (Ryan) don't know the card," which indicates that the suit is spades or diamonds.

Listening to what Benjamin said, Ryan figured out that the suit is spades or diamonds. If the number is 8, there are two 8's (with diamonds and with spades), so Ryan cannot determine the suit of the card. So, the number is either 1, 11, or 12.

If the suit is a spade, two numbers (1 and 11) will be left, so Benjamin cannot be sure which card was selected. If the suit is a diamond, only 12 will be left. So, given this reasoning, Benjamin can determine the identity of the card. Therefore, Ryan chose a 12 of diamonds.

1

Ⓐ Who is lying? : Carl

Does the restaurant offer a free dessert today? :
Yes

Ⓑ Card 1

Ⓒ Timmy

How to Think and Solve

1

Ⓐ Abe, Brad, Carl and David line up in alphabetical order. So, when you carefully examine the
statements made by the boys, you can determine who each boy claims is speaking the truth
or not.

David: What Brad says is true.
Carl: What Brad says is not true.
Abe: What David says is true.

Since David and Carl are saying opposite
things, one of them is lying.
If David is telling a lie, the statement by Brad
is also a lie. Since there are two liars it does not
satisfy the problem condition.
If Carl's statement is a lie, then what the other
three brothers say is true.

Therefore, Carl is the person who is telling a lie
and the restaurant offers a free dessert today.

Ⓑ You can make a table as shown below and put
an "×" if it's not possible to attach the respective
card to the bag.

Card / Name	Onion Bagel	Cinnamon Bagel	Whole Wheat Bagel
Card 1	×	×	
Card 2		×	
Card 3			

Using the table as a guide, the bag that contains
cinnamon bagels is the only bag to which card
3 can be attached. So, card 2 can be attached to
the bag that contains onion bagels and card 1
can be attached to the bag that contains whole
wheat bagels.

Ⓒ Here's a scenario to evaluate:
If Taffy is saying the truth, Toby is telling a lie
and Toffee is also telling a lie.
Since two mice are lying, Timmy is saying the
truth.
Timmy is saying, "Teddy is lying," so Teddy is
lying. In this case there would be three mice
telling a lie, so this will not satisfy the condition
of the problem.

If Taffy is telling a lie, it's Timmy who ate the
cheese. So, Teddy and Toby are telling the truth.
In this case, Toffee is also telling the truth, but
Timmy is telling a lie. This case matches the
conditions of the problem.

Answers

1

Ⓐ 30 cookies

Ⓑ 4 cm

Ⓒ 9 cm

How to Think and Solve

1 The key to solving this problem is figuring out how to think about both (1) the 1 cm of space that is between the edge of the cookie sheet and the cookies and (2) the 1 cm of space that is between adjacent cookies.

Let's think about a rectangular area that is composed of one cookie, the 1 cm space between this cookie and the edge of the tray, and the 1 cm space between the cookie and the left edge of the tray. (See the drawing given in the problem description and/or focus on the red rectangle in the top left corner of the cookie sheet below.)

When you tile the rectangular area, so the tray holds the most cookies possible, you will see there will be some spaces left, including also the 1 cm space at the bottom edge of the cookie sheet and 1 cm space along the right-side edge of the cookie sheet.

So, after we remove these extra spaces from the total area of the cookie sheet, we need to think about how much area is taken up by one cookie including the 1 cm space that surrounds each cookie. Each side of the square cookie sheet after removing the extra spaces will be 31 − 1 = 30 (cm).

So, to solve this problem, we can think as if we are tiling the rectangular area (a cookie with spaces) on the 30 cm square cooking sheet.

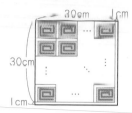

Ⓐ The dimensions of the rectangular area with 5 × 4 cm cookies and 1 cm spaces are
Length: 1 + 5 = 6 (cm)
Width: 1 + 4 = 5 (cm)
So, think of Emily as tiling the 6 × 5 cm rectangles on a square cooking sheet with 30 cm sides. Emily will place the rectangles on the cookie sheet as follows:
in each row, 30 ÷ 5 = 6 cookies per row
in each column, 30 ÷ 6 = 5 cookies per column
Therefore, there are 6 × 5 = 30 cookies on the cookie tray.

[Alternative Solution]
The area of the square cookie sheet without the extra spaces is 30 × 30 = 900 (cm²).
The area covered by one rectangular cookie is 6 × 5 = 30 (cm²)
So, the maximum number of cookies is found by division,
900 ÷ 30 = 30.

Ⓑ Think about the area of a cookie and the 1cm spaces surrounding a cookie as comprising a larger rectangular space. The side of each square is now 1 cm longer than the length of a cookie. We assume Emily is placing these squares on the 30 cm square cooking sheet. On a square cooking sheet, she can put the same number of squares in each row and column, and we see that
36 = 6 × 6
Therefore, she can put 6 cookies in each row and column.
Then the side of each square space will be 30 ÷ 6 = 5 (cm)
And the side of each cookie will be 5 − 1 = 4 (cm).

118

C If you think of a cookie with a 29 cm length and a 9 cm width combined with a 1 cm space, the result is a rectangle that has the following dimensions:

Length: $1 + 29 = 30$ (cm)
Width: $1 + 9 = 10$ (cm)

Then, the remaining space forms the shape of a rectangle with a length of $30 - 10 = 20$ (cm) and a width of 30 cm.
Finally, think of tiling squares (area of a cookie and 1 cm spaces) without leaving gaps. The longest value for the side of the square will be the greatest common factor of 20 and 30, which is 10.
Therefore, the side of the square will be 10 cm, which is the greatest common factor of 20 and 30. So, the length of each side of a cookie is $10 - 1 = 9$ (cm).

Answers

1

A 1 bag, 5 bags, 7 bags and 35 bags
B 5 bags
C 8 bags

How to Think and Solve

1

A Since she will divide 35 cookies into bags with the same number of cookies and without any extra cookies (without a remainder), we use the factors of 35.
So, she will use 1, 5, 7 or 35 bags.

B Since she will divide the same number of cookies and candies without a remainder, we consider only numbers that both 35 and 15 are divisible by. This means we consider only the common factors of 35 and 15.

Factors of 35: 1, 5, 7, 35 (from the problem A)
Factors of 15: 1, 3, 5, 15

So, the common factors are 1 and 5.
Since she will divide the treats into 3 or more bags, the answer is she will use 5 bags.

C The key point to this problem is for you to think about how to use the remainders. You have to notice two important things:

First, remember to subtract the remainders from the respective numbers. After subtracting the remainders, you can divide the remaining numbers without remainders. Since the remainders are 4 cookies and 5 gumballs, consider the following:

cookies: $28 - 4 = 24$
gumballs: $21 - 5 = 16$

119

Since you are going to divide 24 cookies and 16 gummies into bags without any left over, find the common factors of 24 and 16.

Factors of 24: 1, 2, 3, 4, 6, 8, 12, 24
Factors of 16: 1, 2, 4, 8, 16

Now, notice that the remainder numbers must be less than the number of bags. Since the remainders are 4 cookies and 5 gummies, the number of bags Emily used must be more than 6. Since 8 is the only common factor of 24 and 16 that is greater than 6, there will be 8 bags in all.

Answers

1

Ⓐ More than 17 votes

Ⓑ ① More than 9 votes

②

Ring Toss	Fishing	Treasure Hunt
6 votes	5 votes	4 votes
7 votes	6 votes	2 votes
7 votes	5 votes	3 votes

How to Think and Solve

1

Ⓐ Let's think about a case when the Games category has the greatest number of votes, such as 14 votes for Games, 10 votes for Arts & Crafts, and 9 votes for Explorations. In this scenario, Games has the most votes and will be chosen. However, if Games has 14 votes, but Arts & Crafts has 16 votes and Explorations has 3 votes, then Games will not be chosen.
A case when Games is chosen without fail would occur when Explorations does not get any votes at all. Then all votes (33) are split between the Games and Arts & Crafts categories, but Games gets more votes than Arts & Crafts.

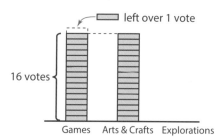

If the votes are split between two categories evenly the result will be 33 ÷ 2 = 16 R1. Therefore, the Games category must receive more than 16 + 1 = 17 votes, in order to win.

Ⓑ ① We are going to think about a case where one of the five games does not get any votes, and the 33 votes are split evenly between the other four games. Now, consider the case where Ring Toss gains one vote more than the other three games (see below).

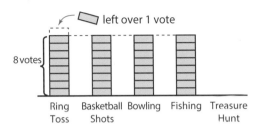

left over 1 vote

8 votes

Ring Toss | Basketball Shots | Bowling | Fishing | Treasure Hunt

So, $33 \div 4 = 8$ R1

Therefore, if Ring Toss receives more than 9 votes $(8 + 1 = 9)$, Ring Toss will be chosen.

② The remaining number of votes, $33 - (10 + 8) = 15$ (votes) will be split among three games: Ring Toss, Fishing, and Treasure Hunt.
Ring Toss, Fishing and Treasure Hunt will compete to gain the remaining votes:
$33 - (10+8) = 15$ (votes).
$15 \div 3 = 5$ (votes)
So, if Ring Toss gains more than $5 + 1 = 6$ votes, Ring Toss will be chosen as the third place.
Since third place has fewer votes than second place which has 8 votes, Ring Toss has 6 or 7 votes.

- If Ring Toss has 6 votes, the rest of the votes will be $15 - 6 = 9$ votes. So, Fishing will have 5 votes and the Treasure Hunt will have 4 votes.
- If Ring Toss has 7 votes, the rest of the votes will be $15 - 7 = 8$ votes. So, either Fishing will have 6 votes and Treasure Hunt will have 2 votes, or Fishing will have 5 votes and Treasure Hunt will have 3 votes.

Ring Toss	Fishing	Treasure Hunt
6 votes	5 votes	4 votes
7 votes	6 votes	2 votes
7 votes	5 votes	3 votes

Answers

1

Ⓐ ① More than 29 votes   ② Yes

Ⓑ [Example]
The number of votes left to count at this point is: $525 - 89 - 45 - 138 - 162 = 91$ (votes).
Class 2 will have $45 + 91 = 136$ votes in total.
Already Class 4 has 162 votes and Class 3 has 138 votes.
Since 136 votes are less than 138 votes, Class 2 will not have a chance to get 1st or 2nd place.

How to Think and Solve

1 The key point of this problem is that, mid-way through the voting, we know the result of the ballot (vote) count from the interim report; that is, we know the number of votes that have been cast already and for whom the votes were cast.

Ⓐ ① As shown in the table, Class 2 is in first place at the midpoint of ballot counting. In order to compete and gain enough of the un-counted votes, Class 2 must capture a greater number of votes than second-place Class 3. Class 1 has 86 votes so far, as shown in the table. So, Class 1 and Class 3 must also compete to gain the remaining available votes, $525 - 86 = 439$ votes.
In order for Class 1 to capture first place without fail, Class 1 needs to receive $439 \div 2 = 219$ R1. That is, Class 1 needs more than $219 + 1 = 220$ votes to secure 1st place.
Therefore, if Class 2 gains more than $220 - 191 = 29$ votes, Class 2 will stay in first place.

② The number of votes not yet counted when the interim report was posted include:
$525 - (86 + 191 + 142) = 106$ (votes).
If all these votes go to Class 1, Class 1 will receive a total of $86 + 106 = 192$ (votes).

121

192 is 1 more than Class 2's previously reported count of 191 votes. So, if all the remaining 106 votes go to Class 1 and Class 2 does not receive any votes, it is possible for Class 1 to become the 1st place winner.

(B) We are thinking about the possibility for Class 2 to be in 1st or 2nd place, so we can solve this problem using the idea we used previously in problem (A)②. So, we find if we put all remaining votes in Class 2, Class 2 still has a chance to win the 1st or 2nd places.

If your response includes the following two part, you will get 20 points:

- You found the number of available votes remaining and put all the votes into Class 2.
- Even if Class 2 gains all the remaining votes, the number of remaining votes will be less than the votes Class 3 and Class 4 have gotten already.

The calculation method for "It's awesome if you know!" is explained below:

The difference between votes in Classes 4 and 1, and Classes 4 and 3 are 73 votes and 24 votes, respectively.
If you add them the sum will be
73 + 24 = 97 (votes).
There are 91 remaining votes, so it is possible for either Class 1 or Class 3 to have more than the 162 votes that Class 4 has. However, it is impossible for both Classes 1 and 2 to exceed the number of votes Class 4 has. From this, we can determine that Class 4 will hold 1st or 2nd place without fail.

Answers

1 [Example]
Alex : He divided the shape by counting the one matchstick at the very end and then counting the remaining sets of 3 matchsticks (there are 8 sets of 3 matches which each look like a backward "C")
Benjamin : He divided the shape into a square made up of 4 matchsticks and (8 − 1) sets of 3 matchsticks.

2 [Example]
(A) Maritza divided the shape into eight groups of 3×3 counters.

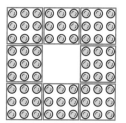

(B) Elle put counters in the center to fill in the shape. She used this larger group of 9 × 9 counters that contains the smaller group of 3 × 3 counters in the center, so she subtracted the 3×3 counters she added to fill in the shape.

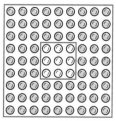

(C) Mario divided the shape into four groups of 6 × 3 counters.

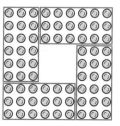

122

How to Think and Solve

1 There are eight groups of 3×3 counters that share one side. You can explain the process by drawing the figures as shown below.

(Alex)

(Benjamin)

If your response includes the points below, it is correct.

- About Alex's solution: You explained the position and number of matchsticks as one stick and (3×8) sticks.
- About Benjamin's solution: You explained the position and the number of matchsticks as four sticks and $3 \times (8 - 1)$ sticks.

---

2 This task requires you to use math strategies to find the number of counters. Let's try to use multiple strategies and to explain simply and clearly! It's very effective to explain our reasoning by using and drawing figures.

If your responses include the two points below, you will get 10 points.

- A clear drawing (figure) that shows how the students divided the counters into square or rectangular groups.
- A clear explanation of how they divided and were thinking about the counters.

1

Ⓐ 314

Ⓑ 33

Ⓒ 665

2

Ⓐ 23.23

Ⓑ 34.65

How to Think and Solve

1

If you can find common numbers, then you can use a calculation strategy. Let's use multiple strategies and properties of calculations to calculate faster and more accurately!

Ⓐ Notice that 3.14 is a common factor in each multiplication portion of the math sentence.

$3.14 \times 14 + 39 \times 3.14 + 3.14 \times 47$
$= 3.14 \times 14 + 3.14 \times 39 + 3.14 \times 47$
$= 3.14 \times (14 + 39 + 47)$
$= 3.14 \times 100$
$= 314$

Ⓑ Notice that $\frac{6}{7}$ and $\frac{9}{7}$ are whole number multiples of $\frac{3}{7}$.

$$\frac{6}{7} \times 43 - \frac{3}{7} \times 45 + \frac{9}{7} \times 12$$

$$= \frac{3}{7} \times 2 \times 43 - \frac{3}{7} \times 45 + \frac{3}{7} \times 3 \times 12$$

$$= \frac{3}{7} \times 86 - \frac{3}{7} \times 45 + \frac{3}{7} \times 36$$

$$= \frac{3}{7} \times (86 - 45 + 36)$$

$$= \frac{3}{7} \times 77$$

$$= 33$$

123

Ⓒ Notice that 7 and 9.5 are common to each multiplication part of the math sentence.

$$7 \times 1.1 \times 9.5 + 9.5 \times 7 \times 3.4 + 5.5 \times 9.5 \times 7$$
$$= 7 \times 9.5 \times 1.1 + 7 \times 9.5 \times 3.4 + 7 \times 9.5 \times 5.5$$
$$= 66.5 \times 1.1 + 66.5 \times 3.4 + 66.5 \times 5.5$$
$$= 66.5 \times (1.1 + 3.4 + 5.5)$$
$$= 66.5 \times 10$$
$$= 665$$

2

Ⓐ If we split 10.1 into 10 and 0.1, we can calculate mental math using a multiplication strategy and property.

$$A \times (B + C) = A \times B + A \times C$$

$$2.3 \times 10.1 = 2.3 \times (10 + 0.1)$$
$$= 2.3 \times 10 + 2.3 \times 0.1$$
$$= 23 + 0.23$$
$$= 23.23$$

Ⓑ The key to solving this problem is to consider using 9.9 as the difference between 10 and 0.1. So, then we can use a multiplication strategy and property.

$$A \times (B - C) = A \times B - A \times C$$

$$3.5 \times 9.9 = 3.5 \times (10 - 0.1)$$
$$= 3.5 \times 10 - 3.5 \times 0.1$$
$$= 35 + 0.35$$
$$= 34.65$$

Answers

1 (1, 6), (5, 2)

2 4

3
Ⓐ ① 1   ② 1
Ⓑ (0, 3), (1, 2)

How to Think and Solve

1 During the conversation with Mr. Ellington and Nathan, Molly came up with a way to investigate the math sentence $A \times B - A = 5$.

When A is 1,
$$B - 1 = 5$$
$$B = 6$$
Since B is a whole number, one of the solutions is (1, 6).

When A is 2,
$$2 \times B - 2 = 5$$
$$2 \times B = 5 + 2$$
$$2 \times B = 7$$
$$B = \frac{7}{2}$$

Since B is a fraction, it doesn't meet the condition of needing a whole number solution.

As we use these processes, we should check when A is one thousand or one million. This will be tedious work.
So, Mr. Ellington hinted that they should pay attention to the letter A that is common in the math sentence.

The following sentence can be transformed, as shown below.
$$A \times B - A = 5$$
$$A \times B - A \times 1 = 5$$
$$A \times (B - 1) = 5$$

124

Now the left side of the final sentence equals a product of A and (B – 1).

The product is equal to 5, and the factors of 5 are 1 and 5.

So, the solution pairs for (A, B – 1) can be (1, 5) and (5, 1).

Therefore, the pair of (A, B) will be (1, 6) and (5, 2).

2 By paying attention to the letter B that is common in the sentence, we can transform the sentence so there is a product of two numbers on the sentence's left side.

$$B \times B - B = 12$$
$$B \times B - B \times 1 = 12$$
$$B \times (B - 1) = 12$$

So, the product of B and (B – 1) is 12.

The factors of 12 are 1, 2, 3, 4, 6 and 12.

Since the difference between B and (B – 1) is 1, the only pair of numbers that meet the condition of (B, B – 1) is (4, 3).

So, B is 4.

3

Ⓐ First, we will pay attention to the common letter A in $A \times B - A$.

$$A \times B - A + B - 1$$
$$= A \times B - A \times 1 + B - 1$$
$$= A \times (B - 1) + B - 1$$

With this common factor (B – 1) can be found, the sentence can be changed:

$$A \times (B - 1) + 1 \times (B - 1)$$
$$= (A + 1) \times (B - 1)$$

Ⓑ Using the result in Ⓐ, the product of (A + 1) and (B – 1) is 2.

Since the factors of 2 are 1 and 2, (A + 1, B – 1) can be (1, 2) and (2, 1).

So, the pair (A, B) can be (0, 3) and (1, 2).

Answers

1

Ⓐ [Example]

We are going to round up the numbers of each month to the nearest thousand, then find the sum:

3,000 + 2,000 + 2,000 + 3,000 = 10,000

The sum of rounded up numbers (10,000 in this case) is greater than the sum of the original numbers. Therefore, the sum of the actual numbers is less than 10,000, so Maria and her family have not saved enough pennies to reach a total of 10,000 pennies.

Ⓑ [Example]

We are going to round down numbers of each month to the nearest hundred, then add to find the sum:

2,900 + 1,800 + 1,500 + 2,800 = 9,000

9,000 is the sum of rounded down numbers that are less than the original numbers.

9,000 is less than the actual sum; so, if we save 1,000 pennies, Maria and her family can reach the total of 10,000 pennies without fail.

2

Ⓐ 5,104   Ⓑ 4,890

How to Think and Solve

1 If we use "rounding up," "rounding down," and "rounding," we can **do simple calculations to** estimate results of **more difficult** calculation problems.

Ⓐ We are going to round up numbers to the nearest hundred.

The sum of the rounded numbers is 10,000.

Since the rounded numbers are greater than the original numbers, it is clear that the sum would not have exceeded 10,000.

If your response includes the following two points, you will get 15 points for each.

- The sum of the rounded numbers is 10,000.
- The sum 10,000 is greater than the sum of the original numbers.

2

(A) First, investigate whole numbers that become 12,300 after rounding:

- When whole numbers are rounded at the tens place: from 12,250 to 12,349.
- When whole numbers are rounded at the ones place: from 12,295 to 12,304

From these findings, you can see that the range of whole numbers that could sum to 12,300 after rounding are from 12,250 to 12,349. We are thinking about the smallest whole number, so the sum of the numbers can be thought of as 12,250.

So, the whole number we want to know can be found by calculating $12{,}250 - (12 + 345 + 6{,}789) = 5{,}104$.

(B) When the quotient was rounded at the tenths place, it became 34.

So, the quotient is more than or equal to 33.6 (≥ 33.5) and less than 34.5.

Since the divisor is 12,

$$33.5 \times 12 = 402$$
$$34.5 \times 12 = 414$$

So, the whole numbers can be more than or equal to 402 and less than or equal to 413. There are 12 whole numbers in this range.

To find the sum of these numbers easily, we will find pairs of two whole number sums to 815, such as $402 + 413$ and $403 + 412$. There are 12 whole numbers, so there are $12 \div 2 = 6$ pairs that sum to 825.

So, the sum of 12 numbers is $815 \times 6 = 4{,}890$

Answers

1 (A) 0   (B) 8

2 82 points

3 [Example]

Take out 0 coins, 1 coin, 2 coins, 4 coins, and 7 coins from each respective bag. Then measure the total weight of the coins on the scale.

How to Think and Solve

1 It is very interesting to find out that mathematics is used for bar codes that we see every day. Be sure you tell your friends and family about how these everyday codes work through a mechanism called "check digit."

Books are coded with a different type of bar code. It is called an ISBN (International Standard Book Number) code. If you are interested in finding out more about the ISBN coding system, you may want to research the mechanism of this code on your own or with your friends.

(A) 491357902468☐

The sum of all odd position numbers starting from the left is:

$$4 + 1 + 5 + 9 + 2 + 6 = 27$$

Three times the sum of all even position numbers starting from the left is:

$$(9 + 3 + 7 + 0 + 4 + 8) \times 3 = 93$$

The sum of 27 and 93 is $27 + 93 = 120$.

The sum of 120 and the check digit is always a multiple of 10. Since 120 is a multiple 10, then ☐ is 0.

(B) 45158☐2603714

The sum of all odd position numbers starting from the left is:

$$4 + 1 + 8 + 2 + 0 + 7 = 22$$

Three times the sum of all even position numbers starting from the left is:

$(5 + 5 + \square + 6 + 3 + 1) \times 3 = (20 + \square) \times 3 = 60 + \square \times 3$

The sum of these two sums is: $22 + (60 + \square \times 3)$

Adding the check digit, 4, makes $22 + (60 + \square \times 3)$ a multiple of 10.

So, the multiple of 10 number is $22 + (60 + \square \times 3) + 4 = 86 + \square \times 3$.

$86 + \square \times 3$ is a number that is a multiple of 10, thus we need to make 4 the ones place of $\square \times 3$. (If the number in the ones place is 4, the calculation of the ones place will be $6 + 4$, so the number in the ones place will be 0.)

Only 8 will make the ones place of ($\square \times 3$) a 4.

So, $\square$ is 8.

You can check your work by putting 8 in the $\square$ space of the bar code above. Then check that 3 times the sum of all even position numbers from the left is $60 + \boxed{8} \times 3 = 84$ and $22 + 84 = 106$. Check the nearest multiple of 10 in 106; it is 110.

$110 - 106 = 4$

This number matches the check digit, 4.

2 The relationships of Karen's, Megan's, and Amy's average test scores can be represented with the line segment model shown below.

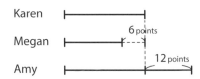

Using this diagram, we can find the difference between Karen's average score and the average score of the three friends.

$(12 - 6) \div 3 = 2$ (2 points)

So, Karen's average score is 2 points higher than the average score of the other three friends. Kimberly's average score is 8 points higher than the average score. Now we can complete the line segment diagram as shown on the next page.

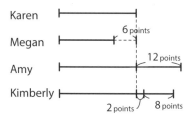

From this diagram, we can find the difference between Karen's average score and the average score of Megan, Amy, and Kimberly.

$(12 + 2 + 8 - 6) \div 4 = 4$ (points)

So, the average score of the four friends is 4 points higher than Karen's score.

Karen's average test score is: $86 - 4 = 82$ (points).

3 You want to take a minimum number of coins from the five bags and use the scale only once to find the total weight of those coins, so you can then determine which bags have the real coins. First, label the five bags, A, B, C, D, and E. We want to take a minimum number of coins out of the bags and weigh them on a scale all at once.

To make it easier to solve the problem, we will think about the case when we do not take any coins from bag A. It can be difficult to think about all 5 bags at the same time, so start thinking about this as a 4-bag problem first.

If we take out 1 coin from bag B and 2 coins from bag C, we should not take 3 coins from bag D, because we cannot distinguish whether bags A and D have fake coins or whether bags B and C have fake coins. Here's the math to show why this would not work.

The weight of a real coin is 10 g, and the weight of a fake coin is 9 g.

The total weight of coins in these 2 cases are as follows:

When bags A and D have fake coins:

$9 \times 0 + 10 \times 1 + 10 \times 2 + 9 \times 3 = 57$ (g)

When bags B and C have fake coins:

$10 \times 0 + 9 \times 1 + 9 \times 2 + 10 \times 3 = 57$ (g)

When the total weight is the same, we cannot determine if bags A and D have fake coins or if bags B and C have fake coins.

Now we are going to think about the problem with 5 bags.

Let's think about taking 0 coins from A, 1 coin from B, 2 coins from C, and 4 coins from D. In this case we should not take 5 or 6 coins from bag E, and here's why.

In the case of taking 5 coins from E:

When bags A and E have fake coins:

$9 \times 0 + 10 \times 1 + 10 \times 2 + 10 \times 4 + 9 \times 5 = 115$ (g)

When bags B and D have fake coins:

$10 \times 0 + 9 \times 1 + 10 \times 2 + 9 \times 4 + 10 \times 5 = 115$ (g)

Because the total weight of the two cases is the same, we cannot determine if bags A and E have fake coins or if bags B and D have fake coins.

In the case of taking 6 coins from E:

When bags A and E have fake coins:

$9 \times 0 + 10 \times 1 + 10 \times 2 + 10 \times 4 + 9 \times 6 = 124$ (g)

When bags C and D have fake coins:

$10 \times 0 + 10 \times 1 + 9 \times 2 + 9 \times 4 + 10 \times 6 = 124$ (g)

Because the total weight of the two cases is the same, we cannot determine if bags A and E have fake coins or if bags C and D have fake coins.

Next, think about taking 7 coins from bag E. The number of coins you are taking from each bag is shown in the following table.

Bag A	Bag B	Bag C	Bag D	Bag E
0	1	2	4	7

If we keep the same number of coins taken out from each bag, we can make an organized table that shows the relationship of two fake bags and the total weight of coins by calculating as we had done before.

Fake Coin Bags	Total weight of coins
A & B	139 g
A & C	138 g
A & D	136 g
A & E	133 g
B & C	137 g
B & D	135 g
B & E	132 g
C & D	134 g
C & E	131 g
D & E	129 g

As you can see in this table, the total weight of coins is different in each two-bag case; that is, none of the combinations have the same weight. By using this table and removing the same number of coins from each, we can identify which two bags have fake coins.

For example, take out 0 coins from bag A, 1 coin from bag B, 2 coins from bag C, 4 coins from bag D, 7 coins from bag E. Then put all the coins on the scale and measure the total weight only once. If the weight of coins is 135 g, then we know bags B and D have fake coins.

This was a very challenging problem. How did you do? Don't you think this idea is fantastic and clever?

Answers

1
Ⓐ 1.85   Ⓑ 15.21   Ⓒ 5.28   Ⓓ 6.16
Ⓔ 9.36   Ⓕ 2.39

2
Ⓐ 13.35   Ⓑ 19.45

3
Ⓐ 0.55   Ⓑ 0.05

4
Ⓐ +, +   Ⓑ −, +

How to Think and Solve

1 Problems Ⓒ to Ⓔ need to be calculated from left to right. For example, in problem Ⓒ, if you calculate 2.45 − 1.07 first, the answer will be wrong.

2 If the calculation uses only addition, we can change the order of addition.

Ⓐ Pay attention to the second decimal place (hundredths) and what order of calculation may be easier to add. If you add 3.43 and 5.57 first, the calculation becomes easier.

$$4.35 + 3.43 + 5.57$$
$$= 4.35 + (3.43 + 5.57)$$
$$= 4.35 + 9 = 13.35$$

Ⓑ If you add 7.72 and 6.28 first, the calculation becomes easier.

$$7.72 + 5.45 + 6.28$$
$$= 7.72 + 6.28 + 5.45$$
$$= 14 + 5.45 = 19.45$$

3

Ⓐ If you think of 0.01 (1 hundredths) as a unit, the answer can be thought as $1 + 2 + 3 + \ldots + 9 + 10 = 55$ (hundredths).

Ⓑ The answer will be the sum of 0.1 − 0.09, 0.08 − 0.07, 0.06 − 0.05, 0.04 − 0.03, and 0.02 − 0.01.

4 There are only four combinations for placing the + and − signs in the two □s, so you may need to use trial and error to find the correct sequence and operations.

Answers

1

Ⓐ 1

Ⓑ [Example]

The 6-digit pattern "142857" repeats starting from the tenths place. The number in the 77th decimal place is 5.

2

Ⓐ 2.85714   Ⓑ 4.28571   Ⓒ 5.71428
Ⓓ 7.14285   Ⓔ 8.57142

How to Think and Solve

1

Ⓐ When you calculate $1 \div 7$ up to the 7th decimal place, it can be represented as below.

$$
\begin{array}{r}
0.1428571 \\
7\overline{)1.0} \\
7 \\
\hline
30 \\
28 \\
\hline
20 \\
14 \\
\hline
60 \\
56 \\
\hline
40 \\
35 \\
\hline
50 \\
49 \\
\hline
10 \\
7 \\
\hline
3 \\
\end{array}
$$

So, the number in the 7th decimal place is 1.

Ⓑ Look at the red shaded parts in the algorithm calculation above. Since the division $10 \div 7$ appears repeatedly, the set of numbers "142857" repeat in the quotient. If your explanation includes this remark, your answer is correct.

$$0.\boxed{142857}\boxed{142857}\boxed{142857}\ldots$$

Then, using this fact, we can easily find the number in the 77th decimal place. Since the set of 6 numbers "142857" continually repeats, we can divide 77 by 6.

$77 \div 6 = 12$ R5

This calculation shows a remainder, so we need to think about what to do with the remainder.

• If the remainder is 1, the answer is 1, the same number as the tenths.

• If the remainder is 2, the answer is 4, the same number as the hundredths.

• If the remainder is 3, the answer is 2, the same number as the thousandths.

• If the remainder is 4, the answer is 8, the same number as the ten-thousandths.

• If the remainder is 5, the answer is 5, the same number as the hundred-thousandths.

• If the remainder is 6, the answer is 7, the same number as the millionths.

Since the reminder is 5, the number in the 77th decimal place is 5.

2 Below are multiplication sentences using the set of numbers "142857" that appear in the quotient of the division problem $1 \div 7$.
The answers are as follows:

Ⓐ $1.42857 \times 2 = 2.85714$

Ⓑ $1.42857 \times 3 = 4.28571$

Ⓒ $1.42857 \times 4 = 5.71428$

Ⓓ $1.42857 \times 5 = 7.14285$

Ⓔ $1.42857 \times 6 = 8.57142$

As Mr. Grant said, the sequence "142857" in the quotient does not change.
Furthermore, if we continue the multiplication sequence above, the product will be $1.42857 \times 7 = 9.99999$.
There are a lot of amazing things to notice about multiplication with the number pattern 142857, aren't there?

Answers

1

*Process of algorithm calculations are omitted.

Ⓐ 43.2   Ⓑ 464   Ⓒ 126

Ⓓ 2808   Ⓔ 60.34   Ⓕ 225.2

Ⓖ 1061.4   Ⓗ 9.024

2

Ⓐ 24   Ⓑ 17.8   Ⓒ 231

Ⓓ 79.8

3 More than and equal to 15 g and less than and equal to 21 g

---

How to Think and Solve

2 When you use the distributive property, the calculations become easier.

Ⓐ $4.5 \times 2.4 + 5.5 \times 2.4$
    $= (4.5 + 5.5) \times 2.4 = 10 \times 2.4$
    $= 2.4 \times 10 = 24$

Ⓑ $8.9 \times 35 - 8.9 \times 33$
    $= 8.9 \times (35 - 33) = 8.9 \times 2 = 17.8$

Ⓒ $2.31 \times 50 + 23.1 \times 3 + 231 \times 0.2$
    $= 2.31 \times 50 + 2.31 \times 10 \times 3 + 2.31 \times 100 \times 0.2$
    $= 2.31 \times 50 + 2.31 \times 30 + 2.31 \times 20$
    $= 2.31 \times (50 + 30 + 20)$
    $= 2.31 \times 100 = 231$

Ⓓ $3.8 \times 5 + 7.6 \times 8$
    $= 3.8 \times 5 + 3.8 \times 2 \times 8$
    $= 3.8 \times 5 + 3.8 \times 16$
    $= 3.8 \times (5 + 16) = 3.8 \times 21 = 79.8$

3 The problem involves inequality.
The weight of a marble is more than 2.5 g and less than 3.5 g. So the case when the total weight of 6 marbles is lightest will be more than $2.5 \times 6 = 15$ (g). The case when the total weight of 6 mables is the heaviest will be less than $3.5 \times 6 = 21$ (g).

Therefore, the weight of 6 marbles falls within the range of more than 15 g (least) and less than 21 g (greatest).

Answers

1

(A) 6   (B) 73.1   (C) 264.6   (D) 66.55

(E) 70.08   (F) 3.075   (G) 19.468   (H) 30.597

(I) 26.2892

2

(A) 55.35   (B) 553.5   (C) 5535

3

(A) 31.4   (B) 723

How to Think and Solve

1 Always be careful about where you place the decimal point.

(A)
```
    3 0
  × 0. 2
    6. 0
```

(B)
```
    4 3
  × 1. 7
    3 0 1
    4 3
    7 3. 1
```

(C)
```
      2 7
    × 9. 8
      2 1 6
    2 4 3
    2 6 4. 6
```

(D)
```
      1 2 1
    × 0. 5 5
        6 0 5
      6 0 5
      6 6. 5 5
```

(E)
```
      7. 3
    × 9. 6
      4 3 8
    6 5 7
    7 0. 0 8
```

(F)
```
      4. 1
    × 0. 7 5
      2 0 5
    2 8 7
    3. 0 7 5
```

(G)
```
      3. 1 4
    ×    6. 2
        6 2 8
    1 8 8 4
    1 9. 4 6 8
```

(H)
```
      4. 3 4
    × 7. 0 5
      2 1 7 0
    3 0 3 8
    3 0. 5 9 7 0
```

(I)
```
      9. 1 6
    × 2. 8 7
      6 4 1 2
    7 3 2 8
    1 8 3 2
    2 6. 2 8 9 2
```

2 Use the sentence $123 \times 45 = 5{,}535$ to reason about and solve these problems that differ by only the placement of decimals. Check how many times more or how many times less the factors are from the factors in the given sentence above ($123 \times 45 = 5{,}535$).

(A) $\frac{1}{10}$ of 123 equals 12.3.

$\frac{1}{10}$ of 45 equals 4.5.

So, the product will be $\frac{1}{10} \times \frac{1}{10}$ or $\frac{1}{100}$ of 5,535.

The product will be 55.35.

(B) 10 times 123 is equal to 1,230.

$\frac{1}{100}$ times 45 is equal to 0.45.

So, the product will be $\frac{1}{10}$ times 5,535.

The product will be 553.5.

(C) $\frac{1}{1000}$ times 123 is equal to 0.123.

1,000 times 45 is equal to 45,000.

So, the product is equal to 5,535.

3

(A) We use a property of multiplication.

$3.14 \times 4.8 + 3.14 \times 5.2$

$= 3.14 \times (4.8 + 5.2)$

$= 3.14 \times 10$

$= 31.4$

(B) We use the fact that 4×25 is equal to 100.

$4 \times 7.23 \times 25 = 4 \times 25 \times 7.23$

$= 100 \times 7.23$

$= 723$

Answers

1 Ⓐ <   Ⓑ >   Ⓒ >   Ⓓ <

2 61.2 cm²

3 Ⓐ 7L 8dL   Ⓑ 77.28 km   Ⓒ 135.24 km

How to Think and Solve

1 The relationship between a factor and product is shown as below:
- When a factor is greater than 1, the product will be greater than its other factor.
- When a factor is 1, the product will be equal to its other factor.
- When a factor is less than 1, the product will be less than its other factor.

Using these facts, let's compare the product and one of its factors.

Ⓐ The factor 0.7 is less than 1.
   So, $6 \times 0.7 < 6$
Ⓑ The factor 1.01 is greater than 1.
   So, $230 \times 1.01 > 230$
Ⓒ The factor 1.9 is greater than 1.
   So, $3.14 \times 1.9 > 3.14$
Ⓓ The factor 0.98 is less than 1.
   So, $2.73 \times 0.98 < 2.73$

2 Given the numbers in this problem, it is easier to find the sum by using the area formula and properties of multiplication than it is to calculate the area of each rectangle and add to find the combined area of the three rectangles.

   Area of a rectangle = Length × Width

So, the sum of the area of three rectangles is:

$$2.7 \times 6.8 + 3.9 \times 6.8 + 2.4 \times 6.8$$
$$= (2.7 + 3.9 + 2.4) \times 6.8$$
$$= 9 \times 6.8$$
$$= 61.2 \ (cm^2)$$

3

Ⓐ There are 15 fish tanks that each hold 5.2 gallons of water.
   So, the quantity of water is $5.2 \times 15 = 78$ (gal).

Ⓑ The car can be driven 13.8km per 1L of fuel. With 5.6 L of fuel, the car can go $13.8 \times 5.6 = 77.28$ (km).

Ⓒ $4.3 + 7.5 - 2 = 9.8$ (L)
   9.8 L of fuel was used between departure and arrival.
   So, the distance traveled was
   $13.8 \times 9.8 = 135.24$ (km)

Answers

1

*Process of algorithm calculations are omitted.

Ⓐ 6.8   Ⓑ 2.7   Ⓒ 0.9

Ⓓ 2.56   Ⓔ 0.56   Ⓕ 0.025

2

*Process of algorithm calculations are omitted.

Ⓐ 0.86   Ⓑ 12.5   Ⓒ 4.84

3 0.4875

How to Think and Solve

1 The method for the algorithm calculation of decimal ÷ whole number is:

1) Start dividing by considering the highest place values in the dividend. Calculate in the same way as basic division with whole numbers until the division gets to the ones place of the dividend.

2) Place the decimal point of the quotient in the same position as it is placed in the dividend.

3) The digits of the partial quotients (recorded below the decimal point of the dividend) are moved down one at a time. Continue the division algorithm process just as with division of whole numbers.

When the dividend is less than the divisor, place zero (0) to the left of the ones place of the quotient and proceed the calculation process described in 2) then 3) above.

2

Ⓐ When you need to divide completely, think about 4.3 as 4.30 by placing zeroes (0's) to the right and continue the division algorithm calculation process.

3 If you represent the unknown number as ☐, the sentence for the incorrect (mistaken) calculation is written as ☐ × 8 = 31.2. The unknown number can be found by dividing 31.2 ÷ 8 = 3.9. The correct anwer is 3.9 ÷ 8 = 0.4875. It may be helpful to realize that the "5" in 0.4875 is in the ten-thousandths place (the 4th decimal place).

If we represent the correct answer as ☐, the unknown number can be represented as ☐ × 8. Thus, 31.2 is 8 × 8 = 64 times as much as ☐. From this, you can find the unknown number as 31.2 ÷ 64 = 0.4875.

Answers

1
(A) 5   R3.9
(B) 4   R6.5

2
(A) (about) 2.7
(B) (about) 25.6

3 16.25 m

4 2.5 times as much

How to Think and Solve

1 After finding the quotient through the ones' place, you need to think about where to place the decimal point in the remainder. The decimal point of the remainder goes in the same place as the decimal point of the dividend. It will be more complicated when doing the calculation (decimal × decimal) and (decimal ÷ decimal), so be sure you fully understand the process of calculating (decimal × whole number) and (decimal ÷ whole number). Fluency with these decimal and whole number calculations will help you immensely in later decimal-decimal calculations.

2

(A) To find a quotient with an approximate number rounded to the two highest places, first find the quotient to the 3rd highest place and round to that number.

(B) To find a quotient rounded up to the first decimal place, find the quotient rounded up to the second decimal place and round the number.

3 The area of a rectangular flower bed can be found by using the formula **Length × Width = Area**. If we represent the width of the flower bed as ☐ m, then ☐ × 2 = 32.5. The length of the flower bed can be found by calculating 32.5 ÷ 2 = 16.25 (m). The problem does not state to what decimal place the quotient should be given, so the division should be done completely.

4 If the length of the yellow ribbon is ☐ times as long as the length of the blue ribbon, you can establish the sentence 46 × ☐ = 115. From this, solve to find the ☐ by calculating 115 ÷ 46 = 2.5 (times as long). If your answer is correct, you might want to think about how many times longer is the blue ribbon than the yellow ribbon. In this case, 46 ÷ 115 = 0.4 (times longer).

Answers

1 $\dfrac{9267}{18534}, \dfrac{9273}{18546}, \dfrac{9327}{18654}$

2 **Math Sentence:** $2400 \div 4 = 600$

$600 + 50 = 650$

Answer: 650 points

How to Think and Solve

1 The relationship between the numerator and the denominator is, as follows:

(numerator) $\times$ 2 = (denominator)

The number in the thousands place of the numerator is 9. So, the ten-thousands place of the denominator should be 1 and the thousands place of the denominator should be 8 or 9. However, 9 is already used for the numerator, so it will be 8.

So, the fraction we are looking for is something like:

$$\dfrac{9\triangle\square\star}{18\blacktriangle\blacksquare\star}.$$

By using the remaining numbers 2 to 7, you make a math sentence $\triangle\square\star \times 2 = \blacktriangle\blacksquare\star$.

Then if you notice that $\triangle$ allows for only a 2 or 3, and $\star$ allows for only 2, 4 or 6, you can find the answer easily.

There are 8 more fractions that equal $\dfrac{1}{2}$ as shown below:

$\dfrac{6792}{13584}, \dfrac{6927}{13854}, \dfrac{7269}{14538}, \dfrac{7293}{14586}$

$\dfrac{7329}{14658}, \dfrac{7692}{15384}, \dfrac{7923}{15846}, \dfrac{7932}{15864}$

2 The points you need to get the whole regular pizza free is $2,800 - 400 = 2,400$ (points) on this special day.

If you think carefully about this, the points you need to get a free half pizza should be $2,400 \div 2 = 1,200$ (points).

However, you need 50 points more than 1,200.

This rule applies for the points of $\dfrac{1}{3}, \dfrac{1}{6}$, and $\dfrac{1}{8}$ sized slices. (e.g., in the case of 1/3 slice: $2,400 \div 3 = 800, 800 + 50 = 850$)

Using this rule, you can find the points you need to get a free $\dfrac{1}{4}$ slice.

Answers

B $\dfrac{1}{20}$ C ① $\dfrac{4}{5}$ ② $\dfrac{9}{10}$ D $\dfrac{12}{13}$

D

$$\frac{2}{3} = \frac{2}{1 \times (1 + 2)} = \frac{1}{1} - \frac{1}{1 + 2} = 1 - \frac{1}{3}$$

$$\frac{4}{21} = \frac{4}{3 \times (3 + 4)} = \frac{1}{3} - \frac{1}{3 + 4} = \frac{1}{3} - \frac{1}{7}$$

$$\frac{6}{91} = \frac{6}{7 \times (7 + 6)} = \frac{1}{7} - \frac{1}{7 + 6} = \frac{1}{7} - \frac{1}{13}$$

How to Think and Solve

1 This problem involves the math concept of partial fraction decomposition.

A This concept is related to finding a common denominator when adding or subtracting fractions with unlike denominators.
The fraction $\dfrac{1}{2}$ is half of 1.

$$6 \div 2 = 3$$

For the first step, you can shade 3 of the 6 parts (three-sixths).

B You need to notice that the denominator of the answer is equal to the product of the two denominators.

C ① Using the idea learned from A and B, the sentence is changed to …

$$= \left(1 - \frac{1}{2}\right) + \left(\frac{1}{2} - \frac{1}{3}\right) + \left(\frac{1}{3} - \frac{1}{4}\right) + \left(\frac{1}{4} - \frac{1}{5}\right)$$

$$= 1 - \frac{1}{5} = \frac{4}{5}$$

② $30 = 5 \times 6$, $42 = 6 \times 7$, $56 = 7 \times 8$, $72 = 8 \times 9$, $90 = 9 \times 10$
So, you can calculate by using the same solution as in problem ① . The given sentence you end up with will be:

$$= 1 - \frac{1}{10} = \frac{9}{10}$$

Answers

1

Ⓐ ① $\dfrac{1}{3} + \dfrac{1}{15}$ ② $\dfrac{1}{6} + \dfrac{1}{66}$

Ⓑ $\dfrac{1}{3} + \dfrac{1}{18} + \dfrac{1}{414}$

*You may add the fractions in any order.

How to Think and Solve

1 This math problem includes a famous story about showing a fraction as the sum of unit fractions.

Ⓐ ① $\dfrac{2}{5} = 2 \div 5 = 0.4$

Next, I find the greatest unit fraction less than 0.4.

$\dfrac{1}{2} = 1 \div 2 = 0.5, \ \dfrac{1}{3} = 1 \div 3 = 0.33, \dots$

So, then we calculate to find the greatest unit fraction less than 0.4.

$\dfrac{2}{5} - \dfrac{1}{3} = \dfrac{6}{15} - \dfrac{5}{15} = \dfrac{1}{15}$

So, $\dfrac{2}{5} = \dfrac{1}{3} - \dfrac{1}{15}$

② $\dfrac{2}{11} = 2 \div 11 = 0.18, \dots$

Then, we will find the greatest unit fraction less than 0.18.

$\dfrac{1}{5} = 1 \div 5 = 0.2, \ \dfrac{1}{6} = 1 \div 6 = 0.16, \dots$

So, $\dfrac{1}{6}$ is the greatest unit fraction less than 0.18.

$\dfrac{2}{11} - \dfrac{1}{6} = \dfrac{12}{66} - \dfrac{11}{66} = \dfrac{1}{66}$

So, $\dfrac{2}{11} = \dfrac{1}{6} + \dfrac{1}{66}$

Ⓑ The greatest unit fraction that will be less than a fraction you have in mind can be easily found by following steps ❶ and ❷ of the process discussed in "How to represent a fraction as the sum of unit fractions."

❶ A fraction you are thinking about converting to a sum of unit fractions is $\dfrac{9}{23}$.
So, $23 \div 9 = 2$ R5.

❷ Since the quotient is 2, the denominator will be $2 + 1 = 3$. So, we can make the unit fraction $\dfrac{1}{3}$.

❸ $\dfrac{9}{23} - \dfrac{1}{3} = \dfrac{27}{69} - \dfrac{23}{69} = \dfrac{4}{69}$

❹ Since $\dfrac{4}{69}$ is not a unit fraction, we repeat the process ❶ through ❸.

❶ A fraction you are converting is $\dfrac{4}{69}$.
So, $69 \div 4 = 17$ R1.

❷ Since the quotient is 17, the denominator will be $17 + 1 = 18$. So, we can make the unit fraction $\dfrac{1}{18}$.

❸ $\dfrac{4}{69} - \dfrac{1}{18} = \dfrac{24}{414} - \dfrac{23}{414} = \dfrac{1}{414}$

❹ $\dfrac{1}{414}$ is a unit fraction.

❺ Since we made unit fractions $\dfrac{1}{3}$, $\dfrac{1}{18}$, and $\dfrac{1}{414}$, so we can write $\dfrac{9}{23}$ as a sum of these unit fractions:

$\dfrac{9}{23} = \dfrac{1}{3} + \dfrac{1}{18} + \dfrac{1}{414}$

138

Answers

1

Ⓐ $\dfrac{27}{10}\left(=2\dfrac{7}{10}\right)$

Ⓑ 1.357

2

Ⓐ $2\dfrac{1}{12}\left(=\dfrac{25}{12}\right)$

Ⓑ $1\dfrac{5}{18}\left(=\dfrac{23}{18}\right)$

Ⓒ $\dfrac{5}{6}$

Ⓓ 3

3

Ⓐ $\dfrac{7}{12}\rightarrow\dfrac{5}{8}\rightarrow\dfrac{47}{72}$

Ⓑ $1.25\rightarrow\dfrac{27}{20}\rightarrow\dfrac{11}{8}$

4

Ⓐ $\dfrac{15}{63},\dfrac{16}{63},\dfrac{17}{63}$

Ⓑ $\dfrac{16}{63},\dfrac{17}{63}$

How to Think and Solve

1

Ⓐ Use $0.1=\dfrac{1}{10}$ and $0.01=\dfrac{1}{100}$ to convert decimals to fractions.
2.7 has 27 one-tenths (0.1's), so $2.7=\dfrac{27}{10}$.

Ⓑ By dividing a numerator by a denominator, you can convert a fraction to a decimal.

$1\dfrac{3}{8}=\dfrac{11}{8}=11\div8=1.375$

2 When calculating addition and subtraction of fractions with unlike denominators, we find a common denominator before calculating.

Ⓐ $\dfrac{3}{4}+1\dfrac{1}{3}=\dfrac{9}{12}+1\dfrac{4}{12}$

$=1\dfrac{13}{12}=2\dfrac{1}{12}$

Ⓑ $5\dfrac{1}{6}-3\dfrac{8}{9}=5\dfrac{3}{18}-3\dfrac{16}{18}$

$=4\dfrac{21}{18}-3\dfrac{16}{18}=1\dfrac{5}{18}$

Ⓒ $2.25=\dfrac{\overset{9}{\cancel{225}}}{\underset{4}{\cancel{100}}}=\dfrac{9}{4}=2\dfrac{1}{4}$

So, $1\dfrac{2}{3}+2.25-3\dfrac{1}{12}$

$=1\dfrac{2}{3}+2\dfrac{1}{4}-3\dfrac{1}{12}$

$=1\dfrac{8}{12}+2\dfrac{3}{12}-3\dfrac{1}{12}=\dfrac{\overset{5}{\cancel{10}}}{\underset{6}{\cancel{12}}}=\dfrac{5}{6}$

Ⓓ $3.6=\dfrac{\overset{18}{\cancel{36}}}{\underset{5}{\cancel{10}}}=\dfrac{18}{5}=3\dfrac{3}{5}$

So, $3.6-1\dfrac{1}{8}+\dfrac{21}{40}$

$=3\dfrac{3}{5}-1\dfrac{1}{8}+\dfrac{21}{40}$

$=3\dfrac{24}{40}-1\dfrac{5}{40}+\dfrac{21}{40}=2\dfrac{\overset{1}{\cancel{40}}}{\cancel{40}}=3$

3 Compare the sizes of fractions by finding a common denominator.

Ⓐ $\dfrac{5}{8}=\dfrac{45}{72},\dfrac{7}{12}=\dfrac{42}{72}$

So, $\dfrac{7}{12}\rightarrow\dfrac{5}{8}\rightarrow\dfrac{47}{72}$

Ⓑ $1.25=\dfrac{5}{4}=\dfrac{50}{40},\dfrac{11}{8}=\dfrac{55}{40},\dfrac{27}{20}=\dfrac{54}{40}$

So, $1.25\rightarrow\dfrac{27}{20}\rightarrow\dfrac{11}{8}$

4

Ⓐ First make the denominators of $\dfrac{2}{9}$ and $\dfrac{2}{7}$ a common denominator of 63.

$\dfrac{2}{9}=\dfrac{14}{63},\dfrac{2}{7}=\dfrac{18}{63}$

Then you can easily compare the size of the fractions: $\dfrac{17}{63}$

$\dfrac{15}{63},\dfrac{16}{63},$

Ⓑ $\dfrac{15}{63}$ can be simplified.

$\dfrac{\overset{5}{\cancel{15}}}{\underset{21}{\cancel{63}}}=\dfrac{5}{21}$

But $\dfrac{16}{63}$ and $\dfrac{17}{63}$ cannot be simplified, because they don't have a common factor.

Answers

1 $2\frac{11}{12}\left(=\frac{35}{12}\right)$ L

2 Maria's house is $\frac{1}{36}$ km farther

3

Ⓐ ① $2\frac{1}{4}\left(=\frac{9}{4}\right)$ ② $\frac{1}{8}$

Ⓑ Takashi $\frac{19}{16}\left(=1\frac{3}{16}\right)$ m

Sam $\frac{17}{16}\left(=1\frac{1}{16}\right)$ m

How to Think and Solve

1 The sum of the amount of milk in bottles A and B can be found by adding fractions with common denominators.

$1\frac{1}{4}+1\frac{2}{3}=1\frac{3}{12}+1\frac{8}{12}$
$=2\frac{11}{12}$ (L)

2 The distance from Nina's house to Maria's house is:

$3\frac{7}{12}+1\frac{11}{18}=3\frac{21}{36}+1\frac{22}{36}$

$=4\frac{43}{36}=5\frac{7}{36}$ (km)

The distance from Nina's house to Anne's house is:

$5\frac{1}{6}=5\frac{6}{36}$ (km)

$5\frac{7}{36}>5\frac{6}{36}$

So, $5\frac{7}{36}-5\frac{6}{36}=\frac{1}{36}$ (km)

The distance from Nina's house to Maria's house is $\frac{1}{36}$ km longer than the distance to Anne's house.

3 The problem involves paying attention to the sum of the two quantities and the difference between the two quantities. Use the diagram wisely and find the length of Takashi's and Sam's tapes.

Ⓐ The difference in the lengths of Takashi's and Sam's tapes is $\frac{1}{8}$ m and the sum of the tapes is $2\frac{1}{4}$ m. So, ① is $2\frac{1}{4}$ and ② is $\frac{1}{8}$.

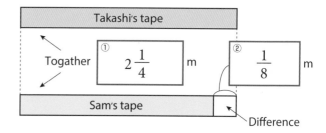

Ⓑ The length $2\frac{1}{4}+\frac{1}{8}$ is the same as twice the length of Takashi's tape. So, the length of Takashi's tape is:

$\left(2\frac{1}{4}+\frac{1}{8}\right)\div2=\left(2\frac{2}{8}+\frac{1}{8}\right)\div2$
$=2\frac{3}{8}\div2=\frac{19}{8}\div2=\frac{19}{16}$ (m)

The length of Sam's tape is $\frac{1}{8}$ m shorter than the length of Takashi's tape.

$\frac{19}{16}-\frac{1}{8}=\frac{19}{16}-\frac{2}{16}=\frac{17}{16}$ (m)

Answers

1

Ⓐ $\dfrac{10}{7}\left(=1\dfrac{3}{7}\right)$ Ⓑ $\dfrac{42}{5}\left(=8\dfrac{2}{5}\right)$

Ⓒ $\dfrac{10}{3}\left(=3\dfrac{1}{3}\right)$ Ⓓ $\dfrac{4}{35}$

Ⓔ $\dfrac{2}{7}$ Ⓕ $\dfrac{5}{8}$

2

Ⓐ $\dfrac{9}{5}\left(=1\dfrac{4}{5}\right)$ Ⓑ $\dfrac{3}{76}$

3

Ⓐ $\dfrac{7}{10}$ m Ⓑ $\dfrac{13}{6}\left(=2\dfrac{1}{6}\right)$ m

How to Think and Solve

1 Fraction × Whole Number $\cdots \dfrac{\triangle}{\bigcirc}\times\square=\dfrac{\triangle\times\square}{\bigcirc}$

Fraction ÷ Whole Number $\cdots \dfrac{\triangle}{\bigcirc}\div\square=\dfrac{\triangle}{\bigcirc\times\square}$

If you can simplify fractions in the process of calculating, the calculations become easier.

Ⓐ $\dfrac{2}{7}\times5=\dfrac{2\times5}{7}=\dfrac{10}{7}$

Ⓑ $\dfrac{7}{15}\times18=\dfrac{7\times\overset{6}{\cancel{18}}}{\underset{5}{\cancel{15}}}=\dfrac{42}{5}$

Ⓒ $\dfrac{5}{12}\times8=\dfrac{5\times\overset{2}{\cancel{8}}}{\underset{5\times7}{\cancel{12}}}=\dfrac{10}{3}$

Ⓓ $\dfrac{4}{5}\div7=\quad=\dfrac{4}{35}$

Ⓔ $\dfrac{8}{7}\div4=\dfrac{\overset{2}{\cancel{8}}}{7\times\underset{1}{\cancel{4}}}=\dfrac{2}{7}$

Ⓕ $\dfrac{15}{4}\div6=\dfrac{\overset{5}{\cancel{15}}}{4\times\underset{2}{\cancel{6}}}=\dfrac{5}{8}$

2 Calculate from left to the right. Convert mixed numbers to improper fractions.

Ⓐ $3\dfrac{3}{5}\times3\div6=\dfrac{18}{5}\times3\div6$

$=\dfrac{18\times3}{5}\div6=\dfrac{\overset{3}{\cancel{18}}\times3}{5\times\underset{1}{\cancel{6}}}=\dfrac{9}{5}$

Ⓑ $\dfrac{12}{19}\div2\div8=\dfrac{12}{19\times2}\div8$

$=\dfrac{\overset{3}{\cancel{12}}}{19\times2\times\underset{2}{\cancel{8}}}=\dfrac{3}{76}$

3

Ⓐ The length of one side of a square can be found by dividing the perimeter by the number of sides (4), or perimeter ÷ number of sides. Squares have 4 equal sides, so the length of a side is:

$\dfrac{14}{5}\div4=\dfrac{\overset{7}{\cancel{14}}}{5\times\underset{2}{\cancel{4}}}=\dfrac{7}{10}$ (m)

Ⓑ The length of one of the sides of the equilateral triangle is $\dfrac{1}{45}$ m longer than the length of the side of the square, $\dfrac{7}{10}$ m.

$\dfrac{7}{10}+\dfrac{1}{45}=\dfrac{63}{90}+\dfrac{2}{90}=\dfrac{\overset{13}{\cancel{65}}}{\underset{18}{\cancel{90}}}$

$=\dfrac{13}{18}$ (m)

The equilateral triangle has 3 sides. So the perimeter is:

$\dfrac{13}{18}\times3=\dfrac{13\times\overset{1}{\cancel{3}}}{\underset{6}{\cancel{18}}}=\dfrac{13}{6}$ (m)

Answers

1

A $\dfrac{11}{12}$

B $\dfrac{38}{9}\left(=4\dfrac{2}{9}\right)$

2

A $\dfrac{15}{28}$ kg

B $\dfrac{45}{4}\left(=11\dfrac{1}{4}\right)$ kg

3

A $\dfrac{6}{5}\left(=1\dfrac{1}{5}\right)$ L

B $\dfrac{14}{5}\left(=2\dfrac{4}{5}\right)$ L

How to Think and Solve

1

A When you multiplied the number by 6, you got $5\dfrac{1}{2}$. So, the number in the □ is found by division.

$$5\dfrac{1}{2} \div 6 = \dfrac{11}{2} \div 6 = \dfrac{11}{2 \times 6}$$

$$= \dfrac{11}{12}$$

B When you divided the number by 4, you got $1\dfrac{1}{18}$. So, the number in the □ is found by multiplication.

$$1\dfrac{1}{18} \times 4 = \dfrac{19}{18} \times 4 = \dfrac{19 \times \overset{2}{\cancel{4}}}{\underset{9}{\cancel{18}}}$$

$$= \dfrac{38}{9}$$

2

A The weight of a bottle can be found by dividing the total weight by the number of bottles.

$$4\dfrac{2}{7} \div 8 = \dfrac{30}{7} \div 8 = \dfrac{\overset{15}{\cancel{30}}}{7 \times \underset{4}{\cancel{8}}}$$

$$= \dfrac{15}{28} \text{ (kg)}$$

B The weight of a bottle is $\dfrac{15}{28}$ kg, so if you have 21 bottles:

$$\dfrac{15}{28} \times 21 = \dfrac{15 \times \overset{3}{\cancel{21}}}{\underset{4}{\cancel{28}}} = \dfrac{45}{4} \text{ (kg)}$$

3 This problem involves adding the same quantity of water $\left(\dfrac{4}{15}\text{ L}\right)$ every day.

2nd day $\left(\dfrac{2}{5} + \dfrac{4}{15}\right)$ L

3rd day $\left(\dfrac{2}{5} + \dfrac{4}{15} + \dfrac{4}{15}\right)$ L

The number of $\dfrac{4}{15}$ L of water added each day increases as shown below.

2nd day → 1 time
3rd day → 2 times …

A On the 4th day, $\dfrac{4}{15}$ L of water will have been added 3 times to the original $\dfrac{2}{5}$ L.

$$\dfrac{2}{5} + \dfrac{4}{15} \times 3 = \dfrac{2}{5} + \dfrac{4 \times \overset{1}{\cancel{3}}}{\underset{5}{\cancel{15}}}$$

$$= \dfrac{2}{5} + \dfrac{4}{5} = \dfrac{6}{5} \text{ (L)}$$

< alternative solution >
The amount of water up to and including the 3rd day was already provided, so all you need to do is add another $\dfrac{4}{15}$ L water for the 4th day.

$$\left(\dfrac{2}{5} + \dfrac{4}{15} + \dfrac{4}{15}\right) + \dfrac{4}{15} = \dfrac{6}{5} \text{ (L)}$$

B On the 10th day, $\dfrac{4}{15}$ L of water will have been added 9 times to the original $\dfrac{2}{5}$ L.

$$\dfrac{2}{5} + \dfrac{4}{15} \times 9 = \dfrac{2}{5} + \dfrac{4 \times \overset{3}{\cancel{9}}}{\underset{5}{\cancel{15}}}$$

$$= \dfrac{2}{5} + \dfrac{12}{5} = \dfrac{14}{5} \text{ (L)}$$

Answers

1

Ⓐ $\dfrac{7}{26}$

Ⓑ $\dfrac{41}{35}\left(=1\dfrac{6}{35}\right)$

Ⓒ $\dfrac{17}{15}\left(=1\dfrac{2}{15}\right)$

Ⓓ 14

2

Ⓐ $\dfrac{13}{18}$

Ⓑ $\dfrac{4}{51}$

Ⓒ $\dfrac{1}{12}$

3 $\dfrac{2}{5}$

How to Think and Solve

1 Calculate multiplication and division first.

Ⓐ $2\dfrac{6}{13} \div 2 - \dfrac{25}{26}$

$= \dfrac{32}{13} \div 2 - \dfrac{25}{26}$

$= \dfrac{32}{26} - \dfrac{25}{26} = \dfrac{7}{26}$

Ⓑ $\dfrac{3}{5} + \dfrac{2}{7} \times 2$

$= \dfrac{3}{5} + \dfrac{4}{7} = \dfrac{21}{35} + \dfrac{20}{35} = \dfrac{41}{35}$

Ⓒ $\dfrac{5}{9} + \dfrac{1}{6} \times 4 - \dfrac{8}{15} \div 6$

$= \dfrac{5}{9} + \dfrac{\overset{2}{4}}{\underset{3}{6}} - \dfrac{\overset{4}{8}}{15 \times \underset{3}{6}}$

$= \dfrac{25}{45} + \dfrac{30}{45} - \dfrac{4}{45} = \dfrac{\overset{17}{51}}{\underset{15}{45}} = \dfrac{17}{15}$

Ⓓ $3\dfrac{1}{6} - 2\dfrac{2}{7} \div 8 + 1\dfrac{9}{14} \times 7 - \dfrac{8}{21}$

$= \dfrac{19}{6} - \dfrac{\overset{2}{16}}{7 \times \underset{1}{8}} + \dfrac{23 \times \overset{1}{7}}{\underset{2}{14}} - \dfrac{8}{21}$

$= \dfrac{133}{42} - \dfrac{12}{42} + \dfrac{483}{42} - \dfrac{16}{42}$

$= \dfrac{\overset{14}{588}}{\underset{1}{42}} = 14$

2

Ⓐ $\dfrac{3}{4} - \left(\dfrac{4}{9} - \dfrac{5}{12}\right)$

$= \dfrac{27}{36} - \dfrac{1}{36} = \dfrac{\overset{13}{26}}{\underset{18}{36}} = \dfrac{13}{18}$

Ⓑ $\dfrac{8}{17} \div \left(6\dfrac{1}{4} - \dfrac{1}{24} \times 6\right)$

$= \dfrac{8}{17} \div \left(6\dfrac{1}{4} - \dfrac{\overset{1}{6}}{\underset{4}{24}}\right)$

$= \dfrac{8}{17} \div 6 = \dfrac{\overset{4}{8}}{17 \times \underset{3}{6}} = \dfrac{4}{51}$

Ⓒ $2 - \left(4\dfrac{2}{5} \div 6 - \dfrac{7}{20}\right) \times 5$

$= 2 - \left(\dfrac{\overset{11}{22}}{5 \times \underset{3}{6}} - \dfrac{7}{20}\right) \times 5$

$= 2 - \left(\dfrac{44}{60} - \dfrac{21}{60}\right) \times 5$

$= 2 - \dfrac{23}{60} \times 5 = 2 - \dfrac{23 \times \overset{1}{5}}{\underset{12}{60}}$

$= \dfrac{24}{12} - \dfrac{23}{12} = \dfrac{1}{12}$

3

$$\left(\dfrac{4}{7} + \boxed{} \times 2\right) \div 8 = \dfrac{6}{35}$$

$(2) \div 8 = \dfrac{6}{35}$, so (2) is $\dfrac{6}{35} \times 8 = \dfrac{48}{35}$

$\dfrac{4}{7} + (1) = \dfrac{48}{35}$, so (1) is

$\dfrac{48}{35} - \dfrac{4}{7} = \dfrac{48}{35} - \dfrac{20}{35} = \dfrac{\overset{4}{28}}{\underset{5}{35}} = \dfrac{4}{5}$

$\boxed{} \times 2 = \dfrac{4}{5}$

So, $\boxed{}$ is $\dfrac{4}{5} \div 2 = \dfrac{2}{5}$

Answers

1

A $\dfrac{27}{4}\left(=6\dfrac{3}{4}\right)$

B $\dfrac{4}{21}$

C $\dfrac{1}{10}$

D $\dfrac{20}{3}\left(=6\dfrac{2}{3}\right)$

E $\dfrac{9}{7}\left(=1\dfrac{2}{7}\right)$

F $\dfrac{56}{5}\left(=11\dfrac{1}{5}\right)$

2

A $>$ 　　 B $<$ 　 C $>$ 　　 D $<$

3

A 192 g

B $\dfrac{35}{4}\left(=8\dfrac{3}{4}\right)$ kg

How to Think and Solve

1

A When multiplying a fraction times a whole number (fraction × whole number), we multiply the numerator by the whole number and keep the denominator the same.

$$\frac{3}{4}\times 9=\frac{3\times 9}{4}=\frac{27}{4}$$

Problems B and C represent the multiplication of a fraction by another fraction (fraction × fraction). For these problems, we multiply the denominators together and the numerators together.

$$\frac{4}{9}\times\frac{3}{7}=\frac{4\times\overset{1}{\cancel{3}}}{\underset{3}{\cancel{9}}\times 7}=\frac{4}{21}$$

$$\frac{3}{8}\times\frac{4}{15}=\frac{\overset{1}{\cancel{3}}\times\overset{1}{\cancel{4}}}{\underset{2}{\cancel{8}}\times\underset{5}{\cancel{15}}}=\frac{1}{10}$$

D For this problem rewrite the whole number 12 as a fraction $\dfrac{12}{1}$.

$$12\times\frac{5}{9}=\frac{12}{1}\times\frac{5}{9}=\frac{\overset{4}{\cancel{12}}\times 5}{1\times\underset{3}{\cancel{9}}}=\frac{20}{3}$$

E and F

When multiplying with factors that are mixed fractions, we convert mixed fractions to improper fraction.

$$\frac{3}{4}\times 1\frac{5}{7}=\frac{3}{4}\times\frac{12}{7}=\frac{3\times\overset{3}{\cancel{12}}}{\underset{1}{\cancel{4}}\times 7}=\frac{9}{7}$$

$$2\frac{2}{3}\times 4\frac{1}{5}=\frac{8}{3}\times\frac{21}{5}=\frac{8\times\overset{7}{\cancel{21}}}{\underset{1}{\cancel{3}}\times 5}=\frac{56}{5}$$

2 The relationship between product and factor can be represented as follows:
- If one of the factors is greater than 1
  - → the product will be greater than the other factor.
- If one of the factors is 1
  - → the product will be equal to the other factor.
- If one of the factors is less than 1
  - → the product will be less than the other factor.

Using these properties, let's compare products with their factors.

A $1.09>1$ 　 So, $\dfrac{7}{8}\times 1.09>\dfrac{7}{8}$

B $\dfrac{6}{7}<1$ 　 So, $\dfrac{7}{8}\times\dfrac{6}{7}<\dfrac{7}{8}$

C $1\dfrac{1}{6}>1$ 　 So, $\dfrac{7}{8}\times 1\dfrac{1}{6}>\dfrac{7}{8}$

D $\dfrac{7}{8}<1$ 　 So, $\dfrac{7}{8}\times\dfrac{7}{8}<\dfrac{7}{8}$

3

A The price of the electric wire can be found by multiplying the **weight of 1 meter × length**

$$120\times 1\frac{3}{5}=\frac{120}{1}\times\frac{8}{5}=\frac{\overset{24}{\cancel{120}}\times 8}{1\times\underset{1}{\cancel{5}}}=192\text{ (g)}$$

B The weight of the iron bar can be solved by multiplying the **weight of 1 meter × length**

$$3\frac{3}{4}\times 2\frac{1}{3}=\frac{15}{4}\times\frac{7}{3}=\frac{\overset{5}{\cancel{15}}\times 7}{4\times\underset{1}{\cancel{3}}}=\frac{35}{4}\text{ (kg)}$$

Answers

1

A $\dfrac{21}{64}$

B $\dfrac{33}{28}\left(=1\dfrac{5}{28}\right)$

C $\dfrac{40}{3}\left(=13\dfrac{1}{3}\right)$

D $\dfrac{81}{7}\left(=11\dfrac{4}{7}\right)$

E 20

F $\dfrac{19}{18}\left(=1\dfrac{1}{18}\right)$

2

A $\dfrac{512}{27}\left(=18\dfrac{26}{27}\right)\text{cm}^3$

B $\dfrac{13}{4}\left(=3\dfrac{1}{4}\right)\text{m}^3$

3 $\dfrac{14}{5}\left(=2\dfrac{4}{5}\right)\text{dL}$

How to Think and Solve

1

A Even if you are multiplying three fractions, you still multiply the numerators together and the denominators together, exactly as when you multiply two fractions.

$$\frac{7}{8}\times\frac{1}{2}\times\frac{3}{4}=\frac{7\times1\times3}{8\times2\times4}=\frac{21}{64}$$

B $$1\frac{2}{9}\times\frac{3}{7}\times2\frac{1}{4}=\frac{11}{9}\times\frac{3}{7}\times\frac{9}{4}$$

$$=\frac{11\times3\times\overset{1}{\cancel{9}}}{\underset{1}{\cancel{9}}\times7\times4}=\frac{33}{28}$$

C $$\frac{5}{6}\times2\frac{2}{5}\times6\frac{2}{3}=\frac{5}{6}\times\frac{12}{5}\times\frac{20}{3}$$

$$=\frac{\overset{1}{\cancel{5}}\times\overset{2}{\cancel{12}}\times20}{\underset{1}{\cancel{6}}\times\underset{1}{\cancel{5}}\times3}=\frac{40}{3}$$

D – F

When calculating a math sentence that includes a fraction, a whole number, and a decimal number, convert all the numbers to fractions before solving to find the product.

D $$\frac{5}{7}\times18\times\frac{9}{10}=\frac{5}{7}\times\frac{18}{1}\times\frac{9}{10}$$

$$=\frac{\overset{1}{\cancel{5}}\times\overset{9}{\cancel{18}}\times9}{7\times1\times\underset{5}{\cancel{10}}}=\frac{81}{7}$$

E $$27\times\frac{10}{21}\times1\frac{5}{9}=\frac{27}{1}\times\frac{10}{21}\times\frac{14}{9}$$

$$=\frac{\overset{3}{\cancel{27}}\times10\times\overset{2}{\cancel{14}}}{1\times\underset{7}{\cancel{21}}\times\underset{1}{\cancel{9}}}=20$$

F $$2\frac{2}{3}\times0.125\times3\frac{1}{6}=\frac{8}{3}\times\frac{1}{8}\times\frac{19}{6}$$

$$=\frac{\overset{1}{\cancel{8}}\times1\times19}{3\times\underset{1}{\cancel{8}}\times6}=\frac{19}{18}$$

2

A The formula for the volume of a cube is:

Volume of a cube = Side length × Side length × Side length

$$2\frac{2}{3}\times2\frac{2}{3}\times2\frac{2}{3}=\frac{8\times8\times8}{3\times3\times3}=\frac{512}{27}\;(\text{cm}^3)$$

B The formula for the volume of a rectangular prism is:

Volume of a rectangular prism = Length × Width × Height

$$\frac{3}{4}\times3\times1\frac{4}{9}=\frac{3}{4}\times\frac{3}{1}\times\frac{13}{9}$$

$$=\frac{\overset{1}{\cancel{3}}\times\overset{1}{\cancel{3}}\times13}{4\times1\times\underset{3}{\cancel{9}}}=\frac{13}{4}\;(\text{m}^3)$$

3 The quantity of paint needed to paint the wall can be solved by multiplying

Quantity of paint needed to paint the wall of 1 m² × Area to be painted

$\dfrac{2}{3}$ dL of paint is needed to paint the wall of 1 m² and the area of the wall is $1.5\times2\dfrac{4}{5}$ m²; so, the paint you need to paint the wall is:

$$\frac{2}{3}\times\left(1.5\times2\frac{4}{5}\right)=\frac{2}{3}\times\frac{3}{2}\times\frac{14}{5}$$

$$=\frac{\overset{1}{\cancel{2}}\times\overset{1}{\cancel{3}}\times14}{\underset{1}{\cancel{3}}\times\underset{1}{\cancel{2}}\times5}=\frac{14}{5}\;(\text{dL})$$

Answers

1

Ⓐ [Example]

We can't just add denominators or numerators without making sense of the fractions we are adding. If we don't find a common denominator, then we will be adding parts that are not the same size and the denominator we give to the sum will not make sense. In this problem, the given denominators are 2 and 3. So, use the least common denominator of 6 for each fraction before adding the numerators that have changed to reflect sixths, not halves or thirds.

$$\frac{1}{2} + \frac{1}{3} = \frac{3}{6} + \frac{2}{6} = \frac{5}{6}$$

Ⓑ My friend, you put the decimal point of the quotient in the correct position, but the decimal point of the remainder is in the wrong place. When placing the decimal point in any remainder, be sure it is placed in the same digit place as in the dividend. So, in this problem the remainder is 0.02, not 0.2.

Ⓒ Let's use calculation strategies to solve this problem quickly. We don't need to use the column method algorithm. Instead, let's think about how we can use properties of multiplication to find the answer easily by multiplying by 10.

$2.5 \times 0.27 \times 4 + 2.7 \times 9$

$2.5 \times 0.27 \times 4 = 0.27 \times \mathbf{2.5} \times \mathbf{4} = 0.27 \times 10 = 2.7$
(commutative property of multiplication)

$2.7 + 2.7 \times 9 = \mathbf{2.7} \times \mathbf{1} + 2.7 \times 9 = 2.7 \times \mathbf{(1 + 9)}$

$= 2.7 \times 10 = 27$
(identity property of multiplication)

1 Correct solutions will be clear and easy to understand if you use the following steps when explaining problems to your friends:

1) Check the error or the part of problem your friend doesn't understand.
2) Explain how to think about and make sense of the problem, then your friend should try again to find the correct solution.

Ⓐ First, tell your friend that he/she appears to misunderstand addition of fractions with unlike denominators. This way your friend will understand the error and be able to correct errors like this.

If your explanation includes the following two points, your answer is correct. (15 points each)

1) You mention that your friend made a mistake adding fractions with unlike denominators.
2) A clear explanation of how to correct the error and find the right answer.

Ⓑ In the process of decimal division, you might make mistakes placing decimal points correctly in both the quotient and remainder. Explain where decimal points should be placed. When you point out both the error and the part that your friend solved correctly, he (or she) will be able to understand better.

If your explanation includes the following two remarks, your answer is correct. (15 points each)

1) You mention that your friend placed the decimal point in the remainder in the wrong place.
2) The place of the decimal point in the remainder is correctly identified.

c Focusing on the sentences 2.5 × 4 = 10 and 1 + 9 = 10 , Yang used calculation strategies
○ × △ = △ × ○ and ○ × △ + ○ × □ = ○ × (△ + □) .
If you master calculation strategies, your math skills are reinforced and will improve quickly.

If your explanation includes the following two remarks, your answer is correct. (20 points each)

___

1) The calculation strategies you identify help your friend calculate more simply and accurately.
2) How to use these strategies to calculate easily.

Answers

1
A 432 cm³   B 180 cm³

2
A Name: Hexagonal prism
   Volume: 99 cm³
B Name: Octagonal prism
   Volume: 210 cm³

How to Think and Solve

1
A 9 × 8 × 6 = 432 (cm³)

B When we put together the two congruent quadrangular prisms, a rectangular prism is made. The width of the base of the rectangular prism is:
8 + 4 = 12 (cm)
So, the volume of the rectangular prism is:
6 × 12 × 5 = 360 (cm³)

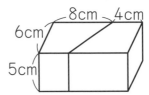

The volume of the rectangular prism above is the sum of the two congruent quadrangular prisms. So, the volume of one of the quadrangular prisms is:
360 ÷ 2 = 180 (cm³)

2
A This polygonal prism has a base with the shape as shown below:

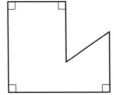

So, this is a hexagonal prism
When we put together the two congruent hexagonal prisms, it becomes a rectangular prism.

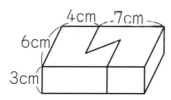

The width of this prism is:
4 + 7 = 11 (cm)
So, the volume of the rectangular prism is:
6 × 11 × 3 = 198 (cm³)
Since this is the volume of two congruent hexagonal prisms, the volume of one of the hexagonal prisms is:
198 ÷ 2 = 99 (cm³)

Ⓑ This prism has a base with the shape as shown below:

Since the base is an octagon, the shape is called an octagonal prism.
When we put together the two congruent octagonal prisms, it becomes a rectangular prism.

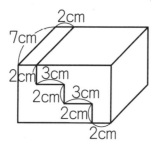

The width of the prism is 2 + 3 + 3 + 2 = 10 (cm) and the height of the prism is 2 + 2 + 2 = 6 (cm).
So, the volume of the prism is:
7 × 10 × 6 = 420 (cm³)
Since this is the volume of two octagonal prisms, the volume of one of the octagonal prisms is:
420 ÷ 2 = 210 (cm³)

Answers

1
Ⓐ Nadine: d
Takeshi: a
Amy: c
Ⓑ 56 cm³

2
Ⓐ 480cm³
Ⓑ 456 cm³

How to Think and Solve

1
Ⓐ In Nadine's solution, we can identify that she divided the solid along the dotted lines, as shown below.

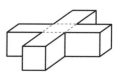

So, the math sentence, (2×3×2) × 4 + (2×2×2), represents Norimasa's solution.

In Takeshi's solution, it is assumed that he subtracted the volume of the four prisms on the corners from the volume of the larger prism drawn with dotted lines, as shown below.

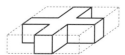

So, the math sentence, (8×8×2) – (3×3×2) × 4, represents Takeshi's solution.

Amy thought about the two long rectangular prisms (as shown below) that intersect to create the cross shape.

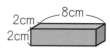

The overlapping part where two prisms are

intersecting creates a cube whose edge is 2 cm. The volume of the center cubic space is counted twice; therefore, this volume must be subtracted one time.

So, the math sentence, $(2 \times 8 \times 2) \times 2 - (2 \times 2 \times 2)$, represents Amy's solution.

Ⓑ By using Nadine's math sentence, the volume of the solid can be found by
$(2 \times 3 \times 2) \times 4 + (2 \times 2 \times 2) = 48 + 8 = 56$ (cm³)
Even if you use Takeshi's and Amy's math sentences, the volume will be the same.

2

Ⓐ The volume of the cube is $8 \times 8 \times 8 = 512$ (cm³)
The hole that runs through the center is a rectangular prism with a base of 2cm × 2cm and a height of 8 cm.
The volume of the rectangular prism is
$2 \times 2 \times 8 = 32$ (cm³)
So, the volume of the solid is $512 - 32 = 480$ (cm³)

Ⓑ The holes are made of the two rectangular prisms whose volume was found in Ⓐ above. However, these prisms are intersecting at the same height inside the cube. Therefore, the volume will be equal to the cross figure that we found in problem **1**. So, the volume of this solid is $512 - 56 = 456$ (cm³)

If the top 3 cm of the solid is cut off, the figure will be shown as below.

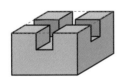

There is another solution. Subtract the volume of two rectangular prisms whose base is 2cm × 2cm and height is 3 cm from the volume of solid that we found in Ⓐ above.
$480 - (2 \times 2 \times 3) \times 2 = 480 - 24 = 456$ (cm³)

There were so many challenging problems you solved in this book. You must have developed strong reasoning and mathematical skills. Z-kai hopes you can see mathematics everywhere in your life and enjoy finding and writing new and exciting problems for your friends and you to solve!

Z-kai Zoom-Up Workbook Math Grade5

■ Authors

Advisory and Editorial Board: Makoto Yoshida, Ph.D.

Dr. Makoto Yoshida is the Director of Curriculum and Professional Development at East West Math LLC, a mathematics education consulting company he co-founded. His service to schools and teachers is comprehensive and presently includes international consulting and professional development for lower-secondary mathematics teachers in Thailand, through the Consortium for Policy Research in Education (CPRE), Teachers College, Columbia University. He served as the president of Association of Mathematics Teachers of New Jersey (AMTNJ) in 2017. Through his work, his interests include helping teachers improve their content knowledge, problem-solving pedagogy, lesson study and instructional use of tools and models, all in the service of fostering students' deeper understanding and avid interest in learning mathematics. Dr. Yoshida earned his Ph.D. from the University of Chicago.

Editorial Staff: Mary N. Leer, Ed.D.

Dr. Mary N. Leer is the director of the educational consulting firm Visualizing Education, Reframing Achievement (VERA): Leer Educational Consulting LLC, and a supervised fieldwork advisor for the Leadership in Mathematics Education program of the Bank Street Graduate School of Education, NYC. Her consulting interests include: editing and writing curricular materials with a special focus on making Singapore and Japanese curricular materials and pedagogy accessible to U.S. teachers; providing professional development for teachers focused on the development of number sense, strategic fluency, and problem-solving pedagogy. The passion that drives her interests is the desire to see the success and joy of learning math come alive for all students. She earned her Ed.D. from Widener University.

■ Z-kai Learning Materials Development Division

First Published on April 1, 2019

Published by Z-kai Inc.
1-9-11, Bunkyo-cho, Mishima-shi, Shizuoka, Japan
E-mail: books-us@zkai.co.jp
Website: https://www.zkai.co.jp/home/corporate/english/index.html

---